FBA

BUILDING AN AMAZON BUSINESS

The Beginner's Guide

Why and How to build a profitable business
on Amazon

Ged Cusack

DISLAIMER

This book is dedicated to my father, Hubert Cusack.

As one of four siblings growing up in Northern England
We never wanted for anything.
While the years of working with Asbestos
and paint fumes have taken a great the toll
on his health.

He has instilled in me an ethos never to give up trying
and allowed me to keep life in perspective
(not sweating the small stuff).

Thank you also to my amazing editors, Jennifer Manson
and Vicki Slade.

CONTENTS

INTRODUCTION HOW TO USE THIS BOOK

HOW TO USE THIS BOOK

When you begin reading this book you may have already started your Amazon business or you may be considering it for the first time. Whatever stage you are at, here are some suggestions on how to use it:

A. If you do nothing else, undertake the "WHY" and "Opportunity cost" exercises. You may decide that an Amazon Business is not for you; if so you will have recouped the cost of this book by not wasting multiple hours and hundreds of dollars on a business you don't actually want.
B. Read the book from start to finish and complete each of the exercises. If you are just starting out on the Amazon journey this book is designed to provide you an overview of the whole process.
C. Read the chapters of the book as you deem you need them and work through just those exercises. If you have already started on your journey you may just want a consolidated reference book.

If you are reading this book you are clearly interested in finding out a little more about starting a business that involves selling on the platform that is Amazon.

There are lots of free and paid resources out there on this subject but the aim of this book is to condense that knowledge and reduce the amount of time you spend ploughing through that cosmos of information.

Apart from all the YouTube videos, blogs and courses (some of which are listed elsewhere in this book) the Amazon Seller Central resource advises exactly how to do the basics. When the processes change, Amazon updates them automatically.

My aim is to provide you enough information to allow you to make some informed decisions. If you decide to proceed with an Amazon business, the profit from the first unit you sell should cover the cost of this book. If you decide not to proceed with an Amazon business then hopefully I have saved you thousands of dollars and hundreds of hours.

My aim is to try and give you some tools to help it become more exciting and less scary.

First the boring disclaimer: (I know most people reading this will take responsibility for their own actions but just in case someone decides that by following some of these suggestions they are not responsible for the outcomes) please read the disclaimer at the start of the book.

Although there are many business ideas and opportunities out there (and some of the information in this book may also be relevant to those) I will focus on the FBA (Fulfilled by Amazon) business.

I'm passionate about seeing people succeed and rather than provide a load of annoying affiliate links I've provided locations and addresses for you to find anything mentioned in this book. It's a book designed to provide benefits for the reader not the author.

We must not lose sight of the fact that (although you may not physically see the stock) an Amazon business is a shop.

You are hopefully finding products that add value to your customers (and that sell).

If we liken your shop to renting premises in a shopping mall, the owners (in this case Amazon) have lots of rules and idiosyncrasies that need to be taken into account.

Just like a shopping mall owner, Amazon can change the terms frequently so this shop isn't as simple as running a market stall.

The simple steps to an Amazon business:

1. Find a product that is selling on Amazon (that meets your criteria).
2. Find a supplier for that product.
3. Sell the product on Amazon.
4. Rinse and repeat.

Right about now you are probably thinking "if that's all it takes, what else do I need to know?"

Although those four steps are the main phases of the system there are lots of intermediate stages to work through, so assuming that you want to learn a bit more, read on.

THE WHY

"He who has a **why** *to live can bear almost any* **how.**" - **Friedrich Nietzsche**

There are many reasons out there for people to do what they do. Even something as simple as getting out of bed in a morning can be driven by our primal need for food or shelter.

Going to your job may be driven by the annual holiday, where you head somewhere nice for a week/fortnight. As long as you are working to live instead of living to work you should have a reasonable balance.

The first question to ask yourself is WHY are you starting an Amazon business?

If you have had any previous experience with Personal Development or courses you may remember being instructed that a strong WHY will help you when you get to the difficult times in any endeavour. Starting an Amazon business is just the same.

You are setting out on the journey to build this business (with no certainty) and in order to have faith in yourself and the system it may help to have that strong WHY to get you through.

EXERCISE ONE DEFINE YOUR WHY (AND PRINT IT OFF)

In order to determine your WHY it is important to focus on your values and determine WHY you undertake any task.

The stronger your emotional WHY, the easier it will be for you to work through any speed bumps in your Amazon business.

There are whole books and courses devoted to setting your WHY (some mentioned in the glossary section at the end of this book) so don't be too disheartened if your first attempt at this exercise doesn't fill you with excitement.

If you work through the WHY exercise and read the next couple of chapters but don't feel your WHY is strong enough, don't let this stop you taking action to build an Amazon business. Avoid Analysis Paralysis.

Assuming you are not looking at building a business just for fun, the main reason you are building an Amazon business is probably what the profits earned will allow you to do; so let's explore that a little more.

STEP 1

1. Pick one major reason WHY you need the funds from an Amazon Business

Some of the reasons why people look at an Amazon business are:

- As a supplementary income

    - To pay for their education.

    - To pay for luxuries (e.g. a sports car or a speed boat).

    - To fund other investment opportunities.

- As an alternative to their current job that they hate (to give them more time flexibility).

- As a stepping stone to a larger investment opportunity.

If you are a parent, there is probably nothing that you wouldn't give for your child's happiness (including a limb or your life). So a WHY of paying for your children's education may work for a parent, but a single teenager would have a different WHY.

Although some people may not be motivated by having more possessions, there is nothing wrong with wanting a better life for yourself. A young entrepreneur may be driven more by fast cars and speed boats.

Whatever stage of life you are at, having a WHY of just wanting to pay your bills may initially seem like a strong driving force; but it can be hard to get passionate about a grocery bill. If you can, find a WHY that is more compelling.

STEP 2

2. If you are finding it difficult to determine a WHY in relation to the benefits of building a business then focus on what would happen if you didn't build a business.

- Imagine the pain of not achieving your goals (e.g. seeing your children's sadness that you missed their performances).

- Now reverse those thoughts by imagining the joy of achieving your goal (e.g. seeing your children's happy face that you attended their performances) and focus on this positive.

There are some schools of thought out there that state that we are motivated more by the avoidance of pain than by thoughts of pleasure. Personally I believe that we gravitate towards what we focus on.

Once you have used this reversal process and determined your WHY, focus only on the positive outcomes.

STEP 3

3. Condense your WHY into a sentence

- e.g. I NEED TO EARN MONEY FROM AN AMAZON BUSINESS SO THAT I CAN QUIT MY CORPORATE JOB AND ATTEND ALL OF MY CHILDREN'S ACTIVITIES

- If you have a huge WHY that you feel you could write a whole book about, distil it down to the strongest sentence (the essence) that inspires your emotions.

- An Amazon business can have large earning potential so don't be afraid to have a huge WHY (funding an orphanage overseas or some other bigger legacy).

STEP 4

4. Close your eyes and repeat that sentence (you created in step 2) at least a dozen times.

- How does it makes you feel?

- Does that sentence excite you?

- If your WHY isn't strong enough to excite you then work through the exercise again.

Anthony Robbins states that "people who have trouble achieving their goals are working off impotent goals". A strong WHY is the driving force for your goals so don't start with an impotent WHY!

STEP 5

5. Keep your WHY with you as your driving force. People have various methods of reminding themselves of their WHY:

- An enlarged version of the sentence in a picture frame (some people keep that frame in their office or bedroom) somewhere prominent.

- Written on a laminated card in their purse/ wallet or somewhere readily available.

- A tattoo of the sentence (this can be a bit extreme and as your WHY may change through life I do advise against this).

STEP 6

6. If you find that your initial WHY isn't strong enough then feel free to utilize any of the following resources to help you refine it:

- "Getting to the Why" – a book by JB Symons.

- "Roadblocks to Goal Setting" – a book (and audio course) by Morris Goodman.

- "Get the Edge" – a seven day audio course by Anthony Robbins.

- "Creating Your Perfect Lifestyle" – a book by Oli Hille.

Although I would ask that you do not wait for the perfect WHY before proceeding to the next chapter (you can refine that later) I would advise having some form of WHY before you proceed.

Just as it's difficult to hit a goal when you don't know what you are aiming at, it can be difficult to remain motivated in any endeavour if you don't know why you are doing it.

Your WHY may change through life which is why the young entrepreneur and the old retiree may have different WHYs.

Employee mind-set

I will cover the issue of your mind-set, from an employee to self-employed (entrepreneur) in the next chapter but I would just like to plant the seed now. Other books on the market may not talk about this issue but I think it is critical to talk about it from the outset, as even a strong WHY will not directly pay the bills.

CHAPTER 1 TAKING STOCK OF YOUR CURRENT SITUATION

Before you embark on your Amazon career, I believe it is important to take stock of your current situation. There are some individuals who will happily just throw themselves into a project without any preparation but there are times when that is not always the best option.

If you are shooting for the stars it might be nice to know if you own a push bike or a rocket ship and if you are about to climb a steep hill it might be nice to know if your back pack is empty or full.

I. People choose to start an Amazon business at various stages in their life:

- Some straight out of college (or instead of college).
- Some when they have had enough of the corporate rat race.
- Some when they are close to retiring and realize they haven't got enough money to survive on.
- Some when they have already retired and realize they haven't got enough money to survive on.

II. Where are you currently at financially and emotionally?

It is up to you to take stock of your own situation and decide not just what your situation is but what you want it to be.

- Are you sick and tired of your current situation with a strong WHY (as discussed earlier)?
- Are you prepared to invest some of your time in a venture (on top of your current job)?

- Have you got some funds to invest?
- Are you time rich but money poor?

Whether you are a budding Mark Zuckerberg (just starting out on your financial journey) or a Colonel Sanders (later on in your life's journey) it could be the right time to start an Amazon business.

I have provided three case studies later in the chapter to give more context of the different stages people find themselves at.

III. What do you want out of an Amazon business?

As we see above, people starting any business may be at various stages of their life but if you are contemplating starting an Amazon business I advise you to start with the end in sight.

Although an Amazon business may not need as much work as a traditional (bricks and mortar) business this may depend on where you see its ultimate destination:

- Do you want an ongoing Amazon business with several product listings that bring in your sole income?
- Do you want an Amazon business with a couple of products as a supplementary income?
- Do you want to use Amazon as a stepping stone to starting your own online business (selling products off your own website, etc.)?
- Do you intend to build an Amazon business and then sell it? There are people currently buying these business (if they meet their criteria).

IV. The Benefits of starting an Amazon business:

- The flexible hours mean that someone with young children can work when the children have gone to bed or someone who is studying can work the business outside of their classes.
- You can start an Amazon business with a lot less capital than a traditional bricks and mortar business.
- You are opening a shop without having to physically hold the stock or distribute it yourself.
- You can get to learn some cool new skills and have new experiences.

V. The drawbacks of starting an Amazon business:

- If you haven't ventured into the online world much there could be a steep learning curve ahead for you.
- The shop doesn't close so you need to have someone available to check the platform daily. This means the flexible hours can be less flexible if you are building the business alone.
- You are very much at the mercy of the Amazon gods (Amazon.com). If they change their terms or they believe you have breached them, they can stop your sales dead.

VI. The opportunity costs

Some people have the money to start the business but are short on time (time poor) and others have the time to start a business but are short on money (money poor).

- If you are "time poor" but have money to invest, the opportunity cost of using your money to invest in an Amazon business is that you reduce the ability to invest that money in another venture that could produce a better return on your investment (R.O.I.)

- o You could be looking at this as an alternative to your current busy job and therefore would be prepared to pay VAs (virtual assistants) to carry out a lot of the tasks involved in starting up, or to buy an existing Amazon business.
- o If you are just looking at this as an investment for your money but do not have the time for another job on the side there may be better investments out there for your money. Even though you are outsourcing tasks, you will still have to input some time into this new venture.

- If you are "money poor" but have the time available to put into building an Amazon business the opportunity cost of using your time in an Amazon business is that you reduce the ability to invest that time in another venture. That other venture could potentially produce a better return on your investment (R.O.I.). There may be easier/more certain ways to exchange your time for income.
  - o If you are married with children and prefer to work evenings and weekends so you can attend your children's sports events, perhaps network marketing could be for you; if you are single and in your early twenties you may want to turn that timetable round, so something like network marketing may not be for you.
  - o You could invest the time in building another form of online business such as blogging or YouTube videos. More time intensive ventures than money intensive, and potentially as lucrative.

VII. Case Study: Simplification of a $10,000 investment

A. If you had $10,000 to invest in a bank account with an annual interest for your money of 5% (I won't discuss tax etc. because everyone has different situations) that's $500 a year for just putting your money in the bank:
   - That's an R.O.I. of 5%.
   - Little risk.
   - No training required.
   - Little/no time required to maintain the funds.

B. If you had $10,000 to invest in a Managed (Hedge) Fund with an annual interest for your money of 10% (I won't discuss tax etc because everyone has different situations) that's $1000 a year for just putting your money into a hedge fund:
   - That's an R.O.I. of 10%
   - A little more risk is involved here as Managed Funds can result in losses as well as profits but being selective about your fund can reduce risk.
   - Some education required (although the sellers of these products will advise you that they are "buy and forget", I suggest reading Anthony Robbins "Money Mastery THE Game" book as it shows that there can be some hidden costs in Managed Funds).
   - As above I suggest you should keep an eye on these investments to maintain the level of your funds.

C. If you had $10,000 to invest in an Amazon business and you could potentially earn $50,000 with an annual R.O.I for your money of 500% (I won't discuss tax etc. because everyone has different situations) that's $39,500 a year more than the first option but here you aren't just putting your money in the bank:

- Some risk (potentially your whole $10,000 stake) although you can reduce the amount of risk by taking some of the precautions in this book.
- Quite a bit of training may be required. You may be able to get another $10,000 but you will never get back the hours you invest in any investment opportunity so always think twice before you commit that time.
- Time required to maintain the funds including:
  - All the stages of this book from finding a product to marketing.
  - Assume 20 hours a week x 52 = 1040 hours.
- The Trade-off for those hours:
  - Assuming our initial rate of $10/hr (x 20 hours a week x 52 weeks) = $ 10,400.
  - With your Amazon business you made the estimated $40,000 profit that's $40,000/ 52 (weeks)/ 20 (hours) this gives you a new hourly rate of approx. $38.50 an hour.

Simplistically put, opportunity cost relates to the risk reward returns.

In example 'A' you are taking very little risk with your funds but receiving very little return (and inputting no time) so the opportunity cost of earning more return is offset by less risk.

In example 'B' you are taking a little more risk with your funds but receiving a bit more return (and inputting some time) so the opportunity cost of a little more return is offset by a little more risk and some of your valuable time.

In example 'C' you are taking more risk with your funds but receiving substantially more return (and inputting substantially more time) so the opportunity cost of using that valuable time (with less risk) to potentially earn more is offset by the fact that you are earning substantially more R.O.I.

VIII.   The Opportunity Cost Exercise

In order to help you determine if an Amazon business (or any investment) is for you, I have devised a simple exercise below.

N.B. We all have different risk thresholds:
- Some people are happy to risk all of their savings in an investment.
- Some people are only happy to risk 5% of their savings in an investment.

If you have a very low risk threshold then building an Amazon business may not be for you.

Although this calculation isn't exact it can hopefully give a snapshot that can help in your decision making. (As per the other Disclaimers in this book please seek professional advice before making any financial investment as this book does not take into account individuals' financial situations).

In order to compare the various costs, certain assumptions are required. If you can get a 10% return or your hourly rate is $100, feel free to substitute these details into your calculations.

- For the purpose of comparison we will use an hourly rate of $10/hour.
- We will assume an annual return of 5% on your savings account (all R.O.I.s will be assumed to be annual).
- Although the general estimate for an expert (in any field) is 10,000 hours we will use 100 hours as an estimate for

competence in a skill you haven't got but need for your business.

- For the purpose of calculations we will use the following values for risk
  - o Low Risk (conservative investment)
    - – 2
  - o Medium Risk (less conservative investment)
    - – 4
  - o High Risk (building a business)
    - – 6
  - o Very high risk (using an untested investment strategy)
    - – 8

EXERCISE TWO CALCULATING OPPORTUNITY COSTS

You are going to input the details into a table so this exercise can be done via spreadsheet, MS Word table or even drawing a table with pen and paper.

I. For any opportunity we will start by completing column A with the annual hours we will require to invest in that opportunity.

II. Now input the amount of cash required to invest in the opportunity into column B.

III. Multiplying the hours (in column A) times 10 to give us a dollar value and add this to the funds required to give you the total investment (put this in column C).

IV. Now input your estimated potential yearly revenue for the opportunity in column D. We are going to use a ball park figure for the potential return on our investment but before you invest any money in an investment I implore you to crunch the numbers in more detail.

V.   You need to determine how risky you view the investment (based on your risk tolerance) but input the corresponding number from the values above into column E.

VI. We are now going to calculate the potential to see if the opportunity is worth pursuing.

    a.   Take the figure **D** divide by **C** divide by **E.**

    b.   Multiply your answer by **100** and round up to the next whole number.

    c.   The final multiplication step is purely to give you some whole numbers (as individuals can more easily visualize whole numbers).

VII. Because you are aiming for a high potential return, if you are receiving a low return on your investment, it is important to recognise that that is stopping you from generating a greater potential return on the same investment (therefore a low return has a higher opportunity cost).

VIII. The higher the potential figure (in column F) the lower the opportunity cost, the lower the figure the higher the opportunity cost.

Opportunity	Hours Req'd ($10/h)	Funds Req'd ($)	Total Investment ($)	Potential R.O.I. ($)	Risk	Potential
	A	B	C	D	E	F
Savings Account	0	$10,000	$10,000	$500	2	3
Hedge Fund	200	$3,000	$5,000	$10,000	4	50
Online Biz	1000	$5,000	$15,000	$100,000	6	111
Your Opportunity						

I have provided three examples below that will hopefully help clarify the process but feel free to run this exercise (by putting your own figures in the blank spaces) for any investment opportunity.

CASE STUDIES

A. Andrew is a college student who wants the money to pay his way through college. He has decided to work in his spare time on an Amazon business rather than getting bar work like a lot of his fellow students. He is computer literate and with an entrepreneurial spirit he undertakes a lot of the tasks himself.
- Andy uses retail arbitrage to turn a $1000 loan from his parents into $5000.
- Andy uses this $5000 to launch two products and ploughing any profits back into his business he soon has 6 products listed on Amazon earning a total of $40,000 a month in profits.

- Andy has repaid the loan from his parents and will continue to build his business into a full blown e-commerce business and is confident that when he graduates he will have a growing concern which will negate him having to go for job interviews.

What are the opportunity costs he has sacrificed here?
- He has sacrificed some time and a small amount of capital.
- As he was money poor he didn't really have money to work for him and hence he sacrificed a bit of extra time.

B. Barbara is a housewife who wants to build an Amazon business on the side. She works part time and (earning $600 a month) she has a goal of quitting her job within 12 months and eventually building the business so that her husband can quit the corporate job he hates. Their initial budget is $5000 and that is all of their savings. They have two young kids and Barbara's husband earns $4000 a month after tax.
  - Although they are investing all of their savings into this venture they are determined to get out of the rat race.
  - Barbara uses this $5000 to launch 3 products (as her husband is also putting some hours into the business) and ploughing any profits back into this business they manage to have 10 products listed on Amazon within the first 12 months.
  - Their monthly profits average out at $75,000 a month.
  - Barbara has already quit her part time job and her husband has reduced his working hours.
  - It takes another 12 months for them to accrue $150,000 in savings and pay off 50% of their mortgage at which stage Barbara's husband quits his job for good.

- They could have quit both their jobs a lot sooner but with two young children and an employee mentality they wanted a big safety cushion before they took the leap of faith.

What are the opportunity costs they have sacrificed here?
- They have risked all of their savings (this also provided a psychological element as it took a while to save that $5000).
- With two young children and both parents working they have also had to forgo some luxuries during this period.
- Very few investments opportunities would have turned the $5000 into a $75,000 a month income in 12 months so the financial opportunity costs are minimal

C. Charlie is a single man in his 50s. He is ex-military with a partial pension of $2,000 a month but that doesn't cover all of his bills, so after completing his military service he took a management job. He is sick of working in the corporate world.
- Charlie is mortgage free and has $100,000 in savings.
- Charlie uses $10,000 of his savings to launch 1 product on Amazon.
- Within 6 months Charlie is earning $5,000 a month from his Amazon listing.
- Charlie chooses to invest very little time to further build the Amazon business and with competition for his product his profits drop off in the next six months.
- Charlie learns from his mistakes and uses another $10,000 to launch two new products.
- Over the next 6 months Charlie builds his Amazon business to list 5 products and is earning $20,000 a month.

- Charlie quits his job and determines to add a further product to his listing each month.

What are the opportunity costs he has sacrificed here?
- Because he only invested a percentage of his savings he was still making some returns on his remaining savings but he reduced those returns in the short run.
- Charlie wasted the first 12 months by not being more focused on his Amazon business and assuming sales would just continue. Although he could have invested that time in another venture, the learnings from that year were also an investment which have paid in the longer term.

1. Reality Check

Although you may read through the case studies and think that starting a business is a no brainer, the opportunity cost calculation is just an overview and doesn't take into account all the other permutations when you are taking a risk.

Let's take a step back to consider some potential downsides.

- In the calculations we have given each risk factor a number but that doesn't take into account actual cash values.
- If you launch your first product and for some reason the stock doesn't sell (e.g. you inadvertently break Amazon's terms and they suspend your listing) you could lose $4,000 of your $10,000 stake.
- Although some issues can be rectified through Amazon Seller support, if the issues are serious (such as suspected trademark, patent or FDA issues) Amazon can be rigid.

- At this stage your WHY better be pretty strong or you may just throw up your arms and quit.
- Now you repeat through the process and when you launch your second product you have issues resulting in another loss (e.g. you have bought your product via wire transfer and your supplier turns out to be a fake).
- If you have now lost another $4,000 out of your initial $10,000 that's 80% in losses.
- If you now have a stake of only $2,000 you need an investment with an R.O.I of 400% just to get back to your initial $10,000.
- If you have taken a long time to build your $10,000 stake then the psychological loss of 80% can be worse than the financial loss.

2. Employee Mind-set

If you are looking at replacing your current job with an Amazon business, there are a few things to take into consideration

The idea of quitting your job may seem both exciting and scary but I would be remiss if I didn't mention the psychological issues with switching from being an employee to running your own Amazon business:

Traditionally when you go on a family holiday (even if you budget) you may still come back with a thousand dollars or so on your credit card. If you estimate that you can pay the credit card bill off in the next couple of pay packets it may not seem like a major issue. If you are self-employed and are just starting out that certainty may not be there.

Even though there are few jobs as an employee that are guaranteed, we tend to remain confident that when we finish work Friday night it will still be there on Monday morning.

When you are an Amazon seller there is always the possibility that Amazon may change their terms or sales may suddenly fall off; so (even with fortnightly payments) the threat of no sales and hence no payments tends to weigh on our minds.

As well as the psychological uncertainty of pay related to your sales (as opposed to an employee pay packet) there is also the issue with planning future events in your personal life.

As an employee it might seem a hassle having to book your holidays six months in advance but if you are relying solely on your Amazon sales income you may not have the certainty that you will have the cash in six months to pay for that holiday.

Weekends can be an issue. If you have a bad week or two of sales you may not feel you deserve to (be allowed to) rest on a weekend and may not enjoy your weekend.

You need to factor in some down time to recharge your batteries and even if you are low on funds there is plenty of free activities you can do without having to sit by your computer monitoring your (low) sales.

In some countries you can get income interruption insurance that will pay your bills (mortgage /rent etc.) should you have an accident but until you have a certain amount of historical data, self-employed people can find it more difficult at the start.

Getting a mortgage can also be an issue when you are not an employee so if you are thinking of purchasing a house you may want to get that sorted before you switch from being an employee to being an Amazon selling business owner.

Depending on your stage of life (and your current responsibilities) you may need to have a large safety net to allow you to rely solely on your Amazon business for your income.

An employee would tend to think that if their Amazon business didn't work out they could always go out and get another job. An entrepreneur would believe that if the Amazon business failed they would just look for another project to create income.

3. Entrepreneur Mind-set

Deciding to be an entrepreneur can be a bit more complicated than turning a switch in your head.

Although you might find some of the ideas below a bit hippy, new age I would say that most highly successful people do some of these activities.

As an entrepreneur you are the one making most (if not all) of the decisions. If you are suddenly moving from an employee position (that includes guidelines) to an entrepreneur state where your actions and their consequences can seem infinite, it can seem a heavy burden.

a) Social giving

Giving (to a charity or social enterprise) helps create an abundance mentality.

Some individuals will give a percentage of their profits to a charity or a social enterprise.

Most entrepreneurs know that these donations are not necessarily selfless as they help an entrepreneur gain an abundance mentality. Isn't giving a great way to be selfish?

Remember you can decide how much and who to give to.

You don't have to let anyone know about your contributions but if you have a symbiotic system where you are promoting the organisation that you are giving to and they are promoting you everybody wins.

Although some people may see attaching a social giving to your business as a marketing ploy I believe that if you give it will come back to you (more an abundance mind-set than just karma).

The trick is to start giving early (even if it's only a small amount).

Many people say they will contribute to charities (or good causes) as soon as they hit a financial goal (like a million dollars in sales). That is the time when they will give a percentage to charity etc.

Very few of these individuals end up giving anything as they either keep increasing the goal or they don't hit that specific goal.

Although it might seem that you need all of your funds to start a business, just starting to give a small amount and increasing that as you grow is a lot easier than waiting to give a large amount.

b) Meditation/Praying
- Whether you are religious, an atheist or class yourself as something else, you need to allot some time to recharge your batteries.
- Meditation can be as simple as sitting for 5 minutes and thinking of nothing.

- Some people meditate, some pray, some play music and I highly recommend that you find the system that works for you.
- It might be that you allocate some time when you first wake up, just before you go to sleep or even at midday. Just closing your eyes and focusing can be all that you need.
- We all have different needs and through trial and error you may find that you need five minutes a week or an hour a day for this recharging.
- Work out what you need and do this for yourself.

c) Anchoring (Overcoming roadblocks).
- As I discussed earlier in the book, you need to have a WHY that allows you momentum and strength to work through the difficult times (road blocks) in your business.
- That Why can be an anchor for you to hold onto when things become difficult

e.g. After a whole week of trying to find the right product you might start to decide that this business is too much trouble, this is one of the times when you need focus on that anchor.

- If you are anything like me, just thinking about an anchor doesn't give me enough support to plough through a roadblock.
- One of the processes that I have used in the past to help that anchoring is Tapping (EFT). This is a simple process that involves tapping meridian points on your body to help you work through mental road blocks.
- Rather than try and abridge EFT or other tapping in this book, I have provided links to free YouTube videos and other detailed explanations of Tapping in the glossary (as this is a print book you will need to type those links rather than click on them).

d) Thinking outside the box.

- Doing whatever it takes is a mantra that most entrepreneurs live by
- When you have expended all of your options you need to look at more options.
- If you have a product that isn't selling and PPC, sales etc. are still not working, what would you do?
  - Liquidate the stock (how would you do that)?
  - Add that stock as an add-on to a different product listing and increase the price of that product?
  - Sell the stock in bulk on Craig's list?

4. Summary

Hopefully this chapter has provided enough food for thought to help you determine if you are prepared to invest your time and money into an Amazon business.

If you feel that you are ready to learn more, please turn over the page and continue the journey.

N.B. The figures in the examples above are just examples and although the returns may seem to be weighted towards starting an Amazon business there are no guarantees.

CHAPTER 2 FINANCIALS AND COSTS

For any business "Cash flow is king" and although I don't want you to feel money is everything, it is the life blood of your business.

The Exercise at the end of this chapter is to set yourself a budget but before we get there I need to provide you an idea of the kind of costs for an Amazon business.

A. What are some of your start-up costs?

1. Education costs
   - There are some free blogs and free courses / e books that can provide valuable information at little or no cost.
   - There is a school of thought that you get what you pay for and although the free sites may provide useful information it may not be as succinct or provide the support of some of the paid courses, such as those supplied by the likes of the Startup Bros and Mark Scott Adams.

2. Time costs to find your products
   - You can pay Virtual Assistants (VAs) to do this, in which case it moves from a time cost to a financial cost.

3. Software purchases to help with product selection (don't purchase any software you don't need at the start) e.g.
   - Jungle Scout (optional).
   - Terapeak (initially you may only need this for a week so look at their 7 day free trial).

4. Amazon seller account (Monthly Fee)
- If you are serious about selling you are going t_ professional seller account (which has a monthly fee).

5. Initial product samples
- You can recoup some of these costs by selling the samples.

6. Initial product stock purchase
- Whether you go for a bigger sample shipment to test on EBay or you go straight to Amazon (Private Label or not) with a shipment large enough for a launch, you need to buy the product before you sell it.

7. Inspection costs (optional)
- If you are purchasing your product from China or overseas (whether you are going to see the stock before it arrives at Amazon or not) it makes sense to get the products independently checked at the factory.
- Although the cost of an inspection (from a company such as V trust) may seem like an unnecessary cost, shipping can cost as much as, or more than, the production costs.
- If your stock arrives in the USA with a critical issue, shipping back to China to resolve the issue may not be a cost (or time) effective option.

8. Shipping costs
- (as discussed in the product selection chapter) these can be prohibitive and even though Chinese manufacturing costs may be cheaper than manufacturing costs in the States, if you choose to use

US suppliers the higher manufacturing costs can be offset by the lower shipping costs.

9. Duty costs

- Depending on the category that your product is classified under the duty costs for import into the USA may vary.
- Some suppliers will state that they include the duty costs in their shipping costs but until your shipment is cleared from customs you can't always be sure of that.

10. Repackaging costs

- Although some people may suggest that you can ship products direct from your Chinese supplier to Amazon, I would suggest that:
  - o The shipping of boxes over the maximum (Amazon limits) of 150 units per carton can be cheaper from overseas so some repackaging will need to be carried out before shipping to Amazon.
  - o The potential pitfalls of a damaged box being refused at an Amazon warehouse mean that there needs to be some allowance for repackaging.
- For US residents there may be the potential for the Amazon seller to receive their shipments from overseas and repackage them themselves (this can move the financial costs to a time cost).
- For overseas Amazon Sellers (who will not physically touch their shipments between overseas suppliers and Amazon Warehouses) they need to have an intermediary [e.g. GWC or FBA inspections] to prepare the boxes prior to shipping to Amazon warehouses.

- If you are outsourcing the repackaging these costs ca. vary depending on the level of preparation or repackaging that you require.

11. Customer Feedback Costs
- If you are wanting organic reviews or want to distribute an e-book with your product, it is worth linking Feedback Genius (or a similar software) to your seller account. The cost of this usually relates to the number of emails sent to customers (so the more you sell the more you will pay) but for only a few cents per email it's worth it.

12. Marketing costs
- Pay Per Click (PPC) – As soon as you have some reviews you will want to promote your product. One of the easiest ways to promote your product is setting up a PPC campaign on Amazon and this will require you to set a daily budget.
- Writing your Listing – Although you can write the text on your listing yourself you may need to subscribe to some keyword search software to optimize your listing. You may determine that for your first listing you will outsource to a VA on Fiverr or Upwork.
- Photo costs – You may be able to take product pictures and edit them yourself (if you're capable) or you may outsource parts of the process. There will be some time or financial costs involved in the pictures for your listing.
- Product launch (potential review discounts) – Although some would suggest that organic reviews are all that you need to list initially a group of reviews will jumpstart your listing. The cost of discount giveaways

is not just lost revenue but there are some Amazon costs per unit you in effect give away.

B. What are some of the Future costs

- Pay Per Click (PPC).
- Facebook Ads.
- Sales Tax Registration.
- Business / liability insurance.
- Income Tax.
- New Product Launches:
  - Even if you have an essential product like toilet paper your costs, margins or competition may make your product no longer profitable down the line.
  - Very few vendors can survive on just one product so you need to be adding products to your inventory if you're going to remain in business.
  - A lot of the costs for your first product launch (and maybe some extras) will be incurred for future product launches.

C. How can you start with very little money – Retail Arbitrage (RA)

- If you have limited funds to start with you may need to increase those funds to launch your first product. Retail arbitrage (RA) can be used to increase your funds to enable you to launch your first product.
  - Simplistically put, RA is buying products on sale (at the likes of Walmart etc.) that are already listed on

Amazon and selling them on Amazon (under those listings) at a profit.

- Tools like the Amazon Seller App allow sellers to check the price of products whilst they are out at the shops and compare the price the item is available for and the price that the item is selling on Amazon (and calculate the potential profit).
- The benefits of Retail arbitrage
- NB at the time of writing this book there is a lot of discussion about the fact that Amazon is not selling items at the best price if the products are available elsewhere cheaper (and to that end I cannot guarantee how long Retail Arbitrage will be available).

D. Financial Pros and Cons of Overseas Suppliers vs American Suppliers

- Simplified examples
  - Item A costs $1.00 per unit manufacturing costs in China.
  - Item A costs $4.00 per unit shipping costs from China.
  - Total cost for Item A is $5.00.
  - Item B costs $6.00 per unit manufacturing costs in USA.
  - Item B costs $1.00 per unit shipping costs within USA.
  - Total cost for Item B is $7.00.
  - Item C costs $6.00 per unit manufacturing costs in USA.
  - Item C costs $0.50 per unit shipping costs within USA.
  - Total cost for Item C is $6.50.

- All things being equal item 'A' looks to be the best option for cost alone.
- Although you may decide when you include other considerations (such as shipping times) that a US manufacturer is the best option, rarely are the costs as close as those in the example; but I have tried to simplify things in order to cater for all levels.

CASE STUDY

I'm including here a simple example of how your first product (s) may go.

Everyone will have their own situation and this is not an exact science so please do not take these figures as a guarantee of a financial return (as with the previous disclaimers, you can lose or make money with any investment so please seek professional advice before making any investment).

We'll call our business owner DAVE (fictional name and does not constitute any real person). Please be aware that the figures below are just to provide an example and may not stack up when you do your own product research for similar items.

1. Dave has worked on his Why and determined that he needs to create some extra income in order to fund his daughter's college education. He has set himself a budget of $5000 (with an extra $1000 credit card available only for emergencies).

2. Dave purchases an online Course on Amazon Selling ($500) and after completing the study he believes he is ready for the next step.

3. Dave carries out his product research and finds three products that he deems meet his criteria
- Product A – A Silicone Baking Tray
- Product B – A Corkscrew
- Product C – A set of Whisky Stones

4. Dave is keen to build fast so rather than pick just one product he decides to try all three.

5. Dave finds suppliers for all three products on Alibaba and orders 10 Samples of each from Chinese suppliers (paying via PayPal. The suppliers provide the samples for free as long as Dave pays for the shipping to his door. As the samples are clearly labelled Samples he pays no Duty on them.
- Product A – A Silicone Baking Tray – Shipping Costs $75.
- Product B – A Corkscrew – Shipping Costs $80.
- Product C – A set of Whisky Stones – Shipping Costs $75.

6. All of the products arrive within a week and although the quality of Products A and B are ok, Product C is excellent quality and Dave's preferred first option.

7. Dave keeps one of each Sample product for reference and lists the other 9 samples of each products on EBay, netting some revenue to offset his initial outlay:
- Product A – A Silicone Baking Tray – Revenue $60.
- Product B – A Corkscrew – Revenue $110.
- Product C – A set of Whisky Stones – Revenue $150.

8. He negotiates with his supplier and they agree to add a Private Label (PL) to the cardboard packaging and the wooden (internal) box that the stones come in.

The PL in this case is a label on the boxes and engraving on the wood: "Stoned on Whisky".

- Dave had the Design produced by a VA on 'Upwork' for $15.
- The first order is for 1000 units and including shipping costs from the supplier is $1500.
- Dave commissions an inspection company in China to check the stock during production at a cost of $300.
- The Supplier is shipping the stones in two cartons each containing 500 units so Dave will have to repack these into cartons of max 150 units when they arrive at his door.

9. Dave has setup his Amazon professional account ($48 a month but first month free) and has created a listing so that he could send the FKNSU code to his supplier (the supplier has agreed to apply the FKNSU code label to the cardboard boxes at no extra cost.

- Dave purchased a group of UPC Codes off EBay to allow him to set up his listing, $10 for 100 codes).
- Dave took photos of his samples using his iPhone and had a VA on Upwork edit the photos and produce a mock-up for the box artwork for the listing – cost $40.
- In order to save time Dave found a Marketing guru who did a keyword search and produced the text for his listing – cost $150.

10. The initial stock arrived at Dave's house in Los Angeles and after repackaging he created a shipping order on his Amazon account and the 7 cartons were shipped to FBA warehouses

- Dave already had some packaging material so no extra costs there.
- Shipping costs Amazon charged to his account $63.

11. Prior to activating his listing Dave sets up Seller labs feedback genius to provide automatic contact with his Amazon Customers ($10 a month).

12. Dave is selling his Stones on Amazon for $20 a set.
- Total Amazon fees are $6 a set.

13. For the Product Launch Dave creates a discount code and gives away 20 Units to friends and family and a further 100 units to review groups.
- Although Dave doesn't earn anything from the sale of these 120 units the small costs per unit mean that his account is $200 in the red.

14. The reviews and Amazons honeymoon period do a great job and in the first 4 weeks Dave sells another 370 units and receives combined payments from Amazon of $4932
- Amazon sales 370 x $14 ($20 Sales price – $6 AMZ fees) = $5180.
- $5180 (Sales Revenue) - $200 (cost of product launch) – $48 (AMZ Monthly fee) = $4932.

15. Dave has now only 510 units in stock and in this example Dave now has enough money from his Amazon payments to order more stock (and potentially order stock of one of the other two sampled products) without adding to his initial budget.

16. Here is a summary table to show the initial budget and costs.

Ser	Expenditure	Amount	Total Expenditure
1	Amazon course	$500	$500
2	Product A Sample Costs	$75	$575
3	Product B Sample Costs	$80	$655
4	Product C Sample Costs	$75	$730
5	Product A Sample Revenue	-$60	$670
6	Product B Sample Revenue	-$110	$560
7	Product C Sample Revenue	-$150	$410
8	UPWORK Designs	$15	$425
9	Initial Stock Purchase	$1500	$1925
10	Initial Stock Inspection	$300	$2225
11	UPC Codes	$10	$2235
12	Photo and Image editing	$40	$2275
13	Feedback Genius	$20	$2295
14	Listing Marketing	$150	$2445
15	Shipping costs within the USA	$63	$2508
16	Amazon monthly costs	$48	$2556

- You can see from the Totals here that $2556 is well within Dave's initial $5000 budget.
- Even if the samples weren't sold that would only be an extra $275 which is still within the budget.
- These calculations do not take into account the amount of time spent on activities such as product research (where you could be carrying out activities that create other income but are designed to give an overview of the initial financial costs involved).
- The figures do not include sales tax etc. either.
- Even if Dave decided that the Amazon business was not for him and he didn't order any further stock his potential profits (less taxes) are:
  - Initial Expenditure $2556

- o Initial Amazon payment $4932
- o Potential further profits $7140 (remaining stock $14 x 510)
- o Total profits = $12072

Approx. ROI = $12072 / $2556 x 100 = **472%**

EXERCISE THREE SET A FINANCIAL BUDGET

Set yourself a financial budget (using the information in the table above as a guideline).

How much money are you prepared to risk in this venture?

You don't need all of the funds at the start. As you will see in the timeline chapter various funds will be required at different stages of the process.

We are just looking at a financial budget here (time required in exchange for potential earnings was covered previously in the opportunity costs).

- How much cash have you got available (including potential credit) and based on the information below is it enough?

- Your budget can take into account potential revenue (from sales) before ordering new stock etc.

- You may decide to launch one product at a time or six but you do need to have an idea if your budget will cover your decision.

NB:

Although currency exchange rates haven't been mentioned here (as most suppliers will accept payment in US Dollars) if you are living in a country where your currency is weaker against the US Dollar your initial outlay may seem large; but as the profits from Amazon are in US Dollars you get an added bonus when the profits are converted into your own currency.

CHAPTER 3 MENTORS, NETWORKS AND EDUCATION

Building an Amazon business is not something that I recommend you do on your own. I am not suggesting that you need to go into a formal partnership with others to build an Amazon business (you may actually be choosing this path because you want to work on your own).

I am suggesting that you dip into the well of knowledge and experience of others in this field and have them accompany you (if somewhat virtually) on this journey.

You can save yourself a lot of time and money by seeking out mentors or networks to help you build your Amazon business. (If you are reading this book you can even classify me as a mentor).

1. Mentors

When someone talks about mentors they usually visualize a teacher who they physically spend time with (acting like an apprentice) to learn from them.

You do not need that intimate relationship as you can extract your mentor's teachings from books and other resources.
- In some endeavours you may research the lives of individuals (now dead) such as Winston Churchill, Colonel Sanders, Amelia Earhart and Indira Gandhi to guide you on your path.
- When it comes to building an Amazon business I would suggest that you subscribe to a specific course, podcast, blog etc. and utilize the time that the authors have already invested to give you guidance and save you time.

- Yes, I know that it can be overwhelming to wade through all the courses and information online which is why I have tried to provide some guidance in this chapter.

2. Networks

Just as your town or city may have a business networking group for a local business, for your ecommerce business an online network can be invaluable to support and expedite your journey.

The two paid courses recommended here have their own Facebook groups. These groups are great as there are hundreds and thousands of other sellers at various stages on the same journey you are embarking on.

Whether you choose to join groups related to the courses I have mentioned or other online groups out there, I highly recommend you get involved as soon as possible.

You will find that these groups have lots of people in the same situation as yourself but also others at various stages along the journey.

As with most relationships, you tend to get out of a network what you contribute so don't join just to take, contribute as much as you can.

As you progress on your journey you will not only benefit from the experience of others on these sites but you will also be able to pay it forward and provide support for others who are not as far along.

a) Here is a list of some of the networks out there (a lot of them are closed groups but you can get access through courses or just asking).

Once again, there are no annoying affiliate links here, have our own preferences, so have a look at any of these and choose what fits you:

- SuperSecret E-Commerce Empire Coaching Community (on Facebook) Over 2700 members
- Amazon FBA Private Sellers (on Facebook) Over 14000 members
- Amazon Private Label Sellers (on Facebook) Over 3000 members
- Scanpower group (on Facebook) Over 13000 members
- Amazon FBA competitive edge (on Facebook) Over 15,000 members
- Jordan Malik's findspotter.com

b) Other Bloggers and podcasts providing info for Amazon Sellers

- Ry Rice Ryan's FBA Journey.com (one of my favourites and a great person) and I recommend visiting her site.
- Nathan Holmquist Amazonmoves.com (visit his site for a free e book).
- Cynthia Stine Fbastepbystep.com
- Jordan Malik Honestonlineselling.com
- Bob Willey Sellercoaching .com

3. Education

There are lots of free courses and blogs out there.

As I am a firm believer in minimizing time I would suggest that the free sites out there are not as concise as a couple of courses I am going to recommend here. I have listed some resources above to give you more variety.

Firstly let me say that I am not receiving any kind of recompense, affiliate fees etc. for mentioning any of these courses blogs etc. My aim in this book is to provide the reader as much value as possible from my experiences on this journey (hence no affiliate links).

I believe that these two courses (which I paid for) both provided me immense value for money and if you choose to undertake them I hope that you get as much out of them as I did.

As I know that the Amazon community has a very wide ranging age group (and financial brackets) I have tried to condense the info down by presenting two courses that will appeal to both ends of the age and money spectrums.

a) The first course I would like to discuss is Mark Scott Adams FBA Headstart course (found at fbaheadstart.com)

Mark is a gentleman who has built many businesses (bricks and mortar and online) over the years.

I have included a link to his course in the resources section of this book (but you can just type in Markscottadams.com as his website contains a detailed bio and info about all of the resources he provides).

The course costs approximately $270 USD (at the time of writing) and once you subscribe you get a login to the site which allows you online access at any time.

The course is laid out on 3 distinct parts

I.   A modular set of videos taking you step by step through the process of building an FBA business.
  • Module 1 is the starting out phase from picking markets and products to dealing with international shipping.

- Module 2 progresses to setting up your Amazon account and your sales page.
- Module 3 takes you through marketing from Pay Per Click (PPC) to Facebook ads.
- Module 4 is about stepping up to the next level, optimizing existing listings and upscaling your business.
- Module 5 is for a smaller (more advanced) group, a VIP level within the course, and allows you to progress even further.

II.   All course attendees have the opportunity to join a closed Facebook group.
- It's great to chat with other people who have completed the same course as you can find (and provide) support on subjects that others may not understand.
- The course is constantly achieving new enrolments so you can rest assured that wherever you are in this process you will find others at the same stage.

III.   A monthly Question and Answer live webinar
- On the monthly call Mark covers common issues or new products that can help course members.
- If Mark finds a useful product he will usually get a representative from the company to provide a demonstration/overview of the product with the benefit that you can ask them questions live.
- The webinars are all recorded and put in the members area so don't worry if your full time job gets in the way of attending a webinar.

b)   The second course I would like to discuss is the Startup Bros - Import Empire Jumpstart Group

Will Mitchell and Kyle Eschenroeder (also known as the Startup bros) are passionate entrepreneurs who have been obsessed with business and the internet since birth.

The course costs approximately $2000 USD (at the time of writing) and once you subscribe you get a login to the site which allows you online access at any time.

Their course is entitled "Import Empire Jumpstart Group" and is laid out in four main parts.

I.   Weekly webinars – twelve scheduled live weekly webinars

The Weekly webinars follow a natural progression taking you from (a newbie) someone who has no idea about building an online business to whatever level you want to achieve (your goals are your limit).

These are full of great information (and can go on for up to 5 hours until everyone's questions have been answered).

Additional to the weekly webinars there are bonus webinars (sometimes one a week) that include experts in the field covering specific topics.

II.   VIP email support

For the period of the course you have access to a VIP email (usually answered within 24 hours but mostly a lot quicker).

On the other end of the email is an ever expanding team of experts in the field of Amazon businesses and e commerce.

This personal service allows you great mentors providing you one on one support throughout the process.

III.   Site Access

Course enrolment gives you a login to the website (which continues after the course) that has a wealth of resources:

a. Webinar Recordings

All Webinars are recorded and the site gives you access to recordings of the webinars (including transcripts of all the questions typed In the webinar).

Previous courses' recordings are also accessible with your membership (including special abridged courses tailored to optimize your business in the Holiday season).

b. Discounted products

As the Jumpstart realm expands (almost 3000 members in their Facebook group alone) they have great buying power and negotiate great discounts for current and past course members.

There is a section in the members' area that provides discounts to lots of tools and resources that ecommerce builders may require.

As new products and tools come onto the market they approach the suppliers (spurred on by their members) and negotiate further deals.

c. Forums

The Forums section is a community and is particularly useful as it is more like a Frequently Asked Questions for newbies.

You can join a mastermind group (or set one up) through the forums.

I find the Facebook group as useful but here you can search for answers without bothering people (when you first start out it can be a bit daunting).

IV.   The Facebook Group

A huge community that has not just course members as participants but lots of the mentors and experts who have contributed to the various courses.

I cannot emphasize enough how helpful the people in this group are and the real sense of camaraderie it promotes.

When you first start out you may see all other Amazon sellers as competition (and in a sense they are) but this is a huge market and the members of this FB group certainly have an abundance mind-set.

As new members are constantly joining the group your question has probably already been asked previously so make full use of the search function on the website.

EXERCISE FOUR YOUR EDUCATION

In the last chapter you set yourself a budget (I do hope you included an Education Fund in there).

As the theme of this book is condensing info it would be wrong of me to have you following hundreds of people (as each teacher has their own different style).

I want you to look at the resources out there (feel free to look at the resources mentioned here and in the resources chapter).

1. Choose two mentors (in the ecommerce field) whose information you will focus on in detail. Remember you are after their information and don't necessarily need to contact them.

2. Choose at least one course (it can be free) that you undertake in the next 30 days.

3. Join at least two networks (Facebook groups etc.) that are focussed on Amazon Selling / e commerce.

4. Read this book to the end (you've paid for it so use it).

CHAPTER 4 SETTING UP YOUR BUSINESS IN THE STATES

The purpose of this chapter is not to give you professional advice on how to set up your business, it is to remind you that this is a business that you are building and give an overview of some of the issues you need to take into account.

1. You need a business plan. I am not talking about a complex 100+ page plan although there are many templates out there. Even if you are writing your plan on a napkin there are some basics that you should have in your plan:
- A Financial plan including:
  - Budget of funds available (this can include potential extra funds).
  - A financial income target (even a rough plan can give you a few milestones) to check if your business is on track.
  - If you want to present your business plan to potential investors the finances will need to be more detailed.
- A structure for your business
  - The Tax structure (you may start small and build an LLC).
  - Who is part of your business (you may be doing it all yourself).
  - Will you at least be using VAs?
- A potential business timetable
  - You can include the timeline exercise (from the next chapter) to provide some ideas to help build this timetable).
- A list of your products

- o This can be criteria for your initial products and can be expanded.
- o Where you have products you need to define the clients for these products.

2. Take into account your own situation

Because people reading this book will be at various stages on their Amazon journey I am not going to go into intense detail about the structure of your business. I will say that you need to get professional advice that suits your current situation.

In some countries you can operate as a sole trader (without registering your business) and in others even registering your business will not provide total protection from litigious actions.

I must emphasize that various countries look at legal entities differently; be aware that if you are trading without any defined business structure you could be liable for any losses or legal issues personally.

A limited company is easier to set up in some countries and this initial cost (depending on your budget) may be advisable to save you a fortune down the line.

Whether Amazon sellers are situated in the United States or overseas they need to individually decide on the structure of their business.

3. Factor in Growth potential.
With approximately 330 million people in the United States and the constant growth of Amazons retail footprint, the market should be big enough for anyone who's starting out in business.

As you start to build your ecommerce empire you may look at other international markets. Your initial simple business plan should have the ability to expand into other markets as you grow.

4. Get an Employer Identification Number (EIN)
When I registered for my Amazon Seller account they required my EIN number. This may change at some stage but until then you will probably need one.

If you live in the United States and you meet the criteria you can currently register for an EIN online:
https://www.irs.gov/Businesses/Small-Businesses-&-Self-Employed/How-to-Apply-for-an-EIN

If you live overseas you need to telephone the United States to register. Follow the same link above to determine the information required during registration (and have the information prepared before you make the call).

5. Sales Tax
Firstly I have to state that I am not licenced or qualified to give specific information on US sales tax but I will give you a quick overview of my understanding and the liabilities below (you must seek legally qualified advice re sales tax and not act solely on this information).

- Various American States have different rules for sales tax, depending on specifics such as Nexus etc.
    - A Nexus, also called "sufficient physical presence," is a legal term that refers to the requirement for companies doing business in a state to collect and pay tax on sales in that state.
    - If you are packing all of your products at home and distributing from home you may be lucky that you only

have one Sales Nexus. Because your home is doubling as the warehouse and distribution centre it is the only place you have a physical presence.

o Amazon have a habit of distributing your stock amongst their FBA distribution centres. Unfortunately if you are using FBA to distribute your products you may have a Nexus in every state that Amazon has a distribution centre.

o Sales tax can be a very complex subject so I highly advise you to seek professional advice.

- You can get Amazon to collect sales tax (for a fee) but before they can collect tax you need to be registered in a state.

o If you register before you make any sales and then you don't have any sales then you have expended funds on tax registration etc. that you could have invested in other products.

o There is a chicken and egg scenario of needing to register before you sell (but not knowing which states you will sell in) so not knowing which states to register in is why you need expert advice.

o I have suggested one company in the resources section who specialize in sales tax but if you have your own advisors feel free to use them (or any others).

- Some people will say don't worry about sales tax at the start but as far as I am aware there is no statute of limitations on this tax so you could be liable for past taxes, penalties and fines (that's not designed to scare you just information that you may find useful).

6. Trade marks

- If you are initially looking to tap into items already selling on Amazon then ensure that the products that you will be selling are not trademarked or patented.
- Some suppliers may have a less stringent view of international trademark and patent law so do your own checking before you order stock of an item.
- You may want to start off by trademarking your company (or brand) if you have a big vision or you may want to wait until your business grows.

7. Brand Registry

- At the time of writing Amazon require you to have a website for brand registry and as this is an added cost when you are first launching you could wait to determine how your product will perform before investing in a website (you may already have a site but I would still not have this as a priority when you first get sorted).
- By becoming brand registered (e.g. if your brand was One Cut for kitchen knives) you are less likely to have other sellers try to hijack your listing.
- As with all the decisions in your business you will need to prioritize and weigh up the risks and rewards and costs here.

8. Frustrations

Unless you are extremely lucky you will hit some speed bumps in your business journey and this can be very frustrating.

You may have some challenges outside of the Amazon Platform such as:

- Suppliers not reaching deadlines.

- Shipments getting lost in transit.
- VAs not meeting deadlines.

You may have some challenges from the Amazon Gods (as I like to call the systems and processes that govern your business on the Amazon platform) such as:

- Stock arriving at an Amazon Warehouse but getting lost in the Amazon system.
- Stock not being available for fulfilment even though it has been showing as available for weeks up to this point.
- Amazon suddenly blocking your account and not allowing you to sell.
- Amazon dispute resolution taking forever.
- Sales suddenly stopping for (what seems like) no reason.
- Someone hijacking your listing.

Keep to your plan and be positive

- All or some of the issues (and some not) listed above may frustrate you at some stage.
- Just remember that there will be others who have (and may be currently) dealing with the same issue.
- Reach out to your network and try to stay grounded.
- Remember that persistence pays off (in most cases).

CASE STUDY

Dave lives in New Zealand and operates as a sole trader (this requires no business registration but he still submits a yearly tax return in NZ).

He downloads the EIN application form from the IRS (United States) website and compiles the information required to file. As he lives overseas he needs to file over the phone so he stays up until 4am one morning and calls the IRS to get his EIN.

Dave contacts a US company (Piesner Johnson) who specialize in sales tax and contracts them to register for sales tax in several US states. Once he has the registration numbers he adds them to his Amazon Seller Account (in order that Amazon can collect sales tax for him).

As part of his business plan he has a VA build a website and as soon as he launches his first Private Labelled product he applies for Brand Registry on Amazon.

Initially he tracks all of his expenses and income on a spreadsheet but part of his plan is to begin using an accounting software (such as XERO) within twelve months.

He has a provisional plan to register as a limited company within eighteen months and to expand into Canada within two years.

EXERCISE FIVE WRITE A BUSINESS PLAN

This doesn't need to be as long as war and peace but should include some of the basics below:

- A Financial plan

- A structure for your business,

- A potential business timetable.

- A list of your products

Some of us are big picture people and some of us are very detailed so try to avoid waiting for the perfect business plan before you start your business.

Most business plans are like a living thing and will evolve with time.

CHAPTER 5 TIMELINES

Although some people are very organized and systematic some of us have more of a scatter gun approach to our activities.

The purpose of this chapter is to help systematize the process for those that want it.

As you work through the process you will suddenly realize that there are some periods (in the process) when there is lots that has to be done, with deadlines, and some periods where the activities don't seem as urgent.

As individuals we are constantly being told to focus on a work life balance but during the initial phases of starting this business you will find some imbalances are necessary.

Phrases like "building a business in your spare time" are just not true! Some of your identifiable time may be unallocated but we all have the same 24 hours in a day.

You may have to sacrifice some of your current activities whilst you start this business (especially if you are building alongside of a full time job) so be prepared for that.

Some people would suggest prioritizing your activities to "Nice to have" and "Critical" (e.g. it is critical to have some pictures for your listing but perfect pictures are a "nice to have").

Of the people who have asked me about the activities involved with starting their Amazon business most have wanted to know what the first steps are.

I have laid out what I see as the natural progression of the process below (and in the case study). This is just my personal preference and you can choose to skip steps or amalgamate them as you please.

1. Deciding on your Why

You can strengthen this Why as you move forward so I am not advocating using defining your Why as a 6 month analysis paralysis. If you haven't already determined a WHY from earlier in the book please revisit this now before you proceed. You must however have some kind of Why to keep you on track when the distractions of normal life arise.

- Certain individuals may be able to do this in five minutes but if you haven't looked at the WHY yet give yourself a day or two for this.

2. Look at the opportunity costs

- By now you should have taken stock of your budget and decided that building an FBA business and the risk versus reward return is in your favour – we'll assume this took a couple of days.
- Just take an hour or so to run the numbers one more time before you invest any of your hard earned cash.

3. Educating yourself

You may feel that you can get enough information from the odd blog or book or even that you need to subscribe to a course.

Before you invest your time and money in a product get a bit of education.

In order to optimize your time you can start a course (learn the basics) and continue your education whilst you undertake the other processes.

- We'll assume you at least take a day to decide on the best product research options and have a plan before diving headlong into the search.

4. Finding your product and your supplier

Depending on your available time this can take anything from a couple of days to a couple of weeks.

We will be generous and give you a week to do this.

5. Ordering your samples

You may find at this stage that the quality of suppliers or the potential margins don't stack up and you have to choose another product so it's back to the previous step.

Once again we are going to be generous and say that you manage to order your samples within a couple of days of negotiation with your suppliers.

6. Waiting for the samples to arrive

This can be one of the most frustrating parts of the process and depending on the number of samples and sizes it can take a week or two.

Whilst you are waiting you can continue with your education and I highly recommend reviewing your skill set and determining what activities you will outsource such as photos, listing your products on Amazon (or EBay if that is your intention for the samples).

This is a great time to create your first listing. You can cancel the listing without it going live but ironing out the kinks before placing your first bulk order is highly recommended, because:

- You will need an FKNSU code if your supplier is putting the labels on your product and (as you need a listing to get the code) the sooner you learn how to create a listing the better you will be prepared.
- Preparing a listing helps you realize potential issues (such as do you need to get ungated in a restricted category) before you order the product.

When your samples arrive ensure you annotate which samples came from which supplier (especially if you are ordering the same item from several suppliers) as this can avoid confusion later.

7. Selling samples

Once the samples arrive you are going to determine whether to proceed with a larger order.

Preferably sell some of your samples on EBay or your overseas equivalent (if you are an overseas seller).

Although you can give products away, by selling the samples you will benefit more by:

- Real customer feedback
- Experience at selling

Ensure that you keep at least one unit of each of your samples to photograph. You will want to get to work on your images in preparation for your listing.

Selling on EBay (etc.) can take a week or two but if you are happy with the quality of your product you may decide to order your first bulk order without waiting for the samples to sell.

8. Placing your first bulk order (Private Label if necessary).

A 21-28 day timeframe from production to the stock landing (at customs) in the United States may be a bit conservative.

*   You may decide to Private Label your product and this may add to the timeframe from placing your order to the production run being completed there.

9. Setting up your account

Amazon has two types of plan when selling on Amazon.com – an individual plan (with no set monthly fee but a fee per item sold and referral fees) and a professional plan (with a set monthly fee and referral fees).

*   With an individual plan rate of $0.99 per item and professional monthly fee of $39.99 it makes sense to quickly graduate to a professional account as (as a business owner) you are intending to sell more than 40 units a month. There are also lots of other benefits for a business owner in a professional plan.
*   In order to give your supplier an FKNSU (for your labels) you will need to set up your seller account and listing to send to your supplier.
*   You do not want to pay fees when you are not selling so how long it takes for first stock production run may determine when you switch to a professional account.

10. Receiving stock and repackaging

If you are shipping stock from China you will want to use the most cost effective method and for smaller quantities and smaller items you may ship via air. To be cost effective with air freight suppliers tend to squeeze as many units as possible in each carton.

- Amazon restricts the contents of the cartons they accept (to a maximum of 150 units per carton) and any carton exceeding 150 units will need to be repackaged before it can be forwarded to an Amazon warehouse.
- Whether you have units shipped to your own premises or have them shipped to an intermediary (for repackaging) this will add additional time in the supply process that needs to be taken into account.

11. Setting up a feedback system

Before your first unit is sold you will want to set up a system to promote feedback from customers (and if necessary to distribute digital products).

- There are software products out there (such as Seller Labs "Feedback Genius") that take very little time to set up and can be added directly to your Amazon Seller account.

12. Product launch

Once your stock is ready to be fulfilled (on sale ready to ship) you need to implement your product launch plan.

- First reviews arrive within 2 weeks of product giveaways and then it is time to push sales through PPC, Facebook Ads etc.

13. Promoting listing

You obviously need to create your listing before you can promote it.

- You can do some promotion for pre-launch reviews before your listing goes live (and your stock arrives) but as soon as the stock arrives in the States your listing needs to be titivated and promoted to death.

14. Reordering stock

Running out of stock post launch is one of the critical mistakes that sellers make.

- With limited funds some sellers need the funds from their initial sales to fund their next shipment.
- It is critical to balance the income from sales against the time required for stock replenishment.

CASE STUDY

Jessica lives in Australia and sets herself a timeline of two months to have her first product sitting on the shelves at Amazon (see the breakdown below).

A. Week One
- Having already taken stock of her current situation she has ran the opportunity costs and determined that she can proceed with this venture with a budget of $5000USD

- She purchases Mark Scott Adams course and watches all the videos (to get an overview of the processes).

B. Week Two
- She undertakes product research and finds a set of pet clippers that meets her criteria.
- She liaises with suppliers and places an order for ten samples.
- Jessica continues to work through the course and familiarize herself with the Amazon processes.

C. Week Three
- The Samples arrive and are thoroughly inspected (5 units are sold on EBay Australia).
- Four units are given away and the recipients will write pre-launch reviews on Amazon.
- A design for the packaging is commissioned on Fiverr (and is received within 24 hours).
- Jessica continues to work through the course and familiarize herself with the Amazon processes.
- Jessica reads through the terms of Alibaba's trade assurance several times, to ensure she understands how the process works.

D. Week Four
- She continues conversations with her supplier to negotiate the best price and refine the product requirements.
- An order for 1000 units of the clippers are ordered (branded as "The Cats whiskers"). The order has been placed through Alibaba Trade Assurance so the payment takes 24hrs to reach the supplier.

- The Suppliers have estimated that the manufacturing process will take approximately 21 days from the order being placed.
- She has set up her Amazon Professional account and created an initial listing to provide the FKNSU code.
- She has used an online barcode creator (to turn the FKNSU code into a barcode) and supplied the barcode to the supplier for labelling.
- She has lodged a Works Order with an intermediary (FBA Inspections) for them to repackage. The Works Order Number has been passed to the suppliers so they can put the details on the cartons.
- Jessica continues to work through the course and familiarize herself with the Amazon processes.
- She contacts an independent inspection company (V Trust) and informs them of her inspection requirements.

E. Week Five
- Jessica continues to work through the course and familiarize herself with the Amazon processes.
- She confirms with the supplier and V Trust that production is on schedule (they are to liaise with each other to schedule the inspection timetable).

F. Week six
- The production run is at approximately 75% and the independent inspection company carry out their inspection.
- The suppliers have dispatched two units (in their packaging) of the new production to Jessica in Australia.
- Jessica continues to work through the course and familiarize herself with the Amazon processes.

G. Week Seven
- The two samples arrive and photographs are taker Jessica's own equipment.
- The photos are sent to a VA in the Philippines for editing (ensuring they meet Amazon's criteria and minimize white space).
- The listing is modified using keywords (from Merchantwords etc.).
- The bulk order is dispatched to the intermediary in California.

H. Week Eight
- The 1000 units arrive in two cartons, clear customs and are delivered to the intermediary.
- The units are counted and repackaged so that they fill six cartons of 150 units and one of 100 units.

I. Week Nine
- FBA inspections confirm that the cartons are now ready for shipment to Amazon.
- Jessica uses her Seller account to create shipping labels for the cartons to be shipped to three Amazon warehouses (as determined by the Amazon system).
- The cartons are shipped to Amazon warehouses using these shipping labels.

J. Week Ten
- The products arrive at Amazon and are (after 72 hours) available for sale.
- The sample testers write the pre-launch reviews.
- Jessica creates codes and gives away 150 discounted codes (units) to review groups.

K. Week Eleven
- The reviewers have now placed over 50 reviews.
- Jessica creates her first PPC Campaign.

L. Week Twelve
- Jessica continues to monitor her PPC Campaign.
- The reviews continue to come in and organic sales grow.

M. Week Thirteen
- Total sales (including discount codes) have exceeded 450 units.
- Jessica now places her second bulk order using her credit card (knowing that by the time the credit card bill is due she will have received enough payment from Amazon sales).

EXERCISE SIX SET YOURSELF A TIMELINE FOR YOUR FIRST LAUNCH

I've provided a case study above to give you some guidance and you can adapt this to meet your own requirements.

Remember:

- The product research period may take longer than you intend but it is time well spent.

- You may be waiting four weeks or so for a product to be ready to fulfil customer orders (so fill that time wisely).

- If you have any time available whilst you are waiting for products try to get ahead with any upcoming tasks.

CHAPTER 6 SKILLS YOU NEED AGAINST PAYING SOMEONE ELSE (FOR THOSE SKILLS)

A lot of self-employed people believe that nobody else can do the tasks better than them, this is partly why they sometimes work a lot longer hours than employees of other businesses.

The fact is when building an Amazon business you are already outsourcing some of the tasks of your business to Amazon and trusting that they can do them.

These tasks include (but are not limited to):

- Customer service (Amazon Seller Central).
- Warehousing (if you are using FBA for distribution).
- Sales tax collection

Although your current financial situation may seem to be the driving factor behind which activities you undertake and which you outsource I believe that each activity should be analysed against your skill set and the opportunity cost of undertaking that activity yourself.

This goes back to categorizing your tasks, your time and your funds.

1. Virtual Assistants (VAs)

In the modern world of business the use of Virtual Assistants (VAs) is becoming more and more common but before you decide if outsourcing to a VA is the right fit for you let's look at what a VA actually is.

A VA is a person or persons that you contract to do specific activities; they are sometimes overseas and you may never meet the assistant in person. Because you may not meet the assistant this is why they are known as Virtual.

The tasks you allocate to these people can be as diverse as photo editing and copy writing to product inspection in China and repackaging in the USA.

If you look on Wikipedia they tend to refer to VAs as "Virtual Office Assistants" but I believe that with modern technology the term now encompasses so much more than office workers.

2. There are several benefits of using a Virtual Assistant from overseas:

- Because the rate of pay is lower in some countries (like India or the Philippines) you can have a highly qualified individual carry out a task at a fraction of the cost in the States.
- With the different time zones you may have someone working whilst you are asleep (and wake up with the task done).
- Because rates are so much cheaper you may be able to pay a team to complete tasks that you could only afford one person to do at home.
- Because Virtual Assistants are independent contractors rather than employees, you are not responsible for any employee-related taxes, insurance or benefits for the VA.

3. There are some downsides to using a Virtual Assistant from overseas:

- Potential language barriers mean that you need to be precise with your instructions / requirements.
- If you allocate a task to a VA and they do not deliver you may miss critical deadlines.
- When you are building a relationship (communications) with a new VA you may have to spend more time explaining and checking the work than if you undertook the work yourself.

4. Activity Analysis

Although we all have our own system of prioritization activities I have listed below some of the questions I ask when determining if I am going to Undertake, Outsource or Delete an activity.

a. Is the activity critical to your business (e.g. creating your listing on Amazon)?
   o If not and it will exceed your budget consider deleting the activity.

b. Do you have the skill set to do it yourself?
   o Even if the answer is yes you may not be as efficient as an Overseas VA at this.
   o Assume a task takes you 10 hours. If you can earn $10/ hour this is costing you $100 in real terms.
   o If a VA can do the task at least as well as you if not better than you for $30 you only have to do 3 hours work to fund this so why wouldn't you outsource this activity?
   o Admittedly you may have to check the work so perhaps we'll allow you an extra hour to check it but once you have built up a relationship with VAs your future tasks can be almost perfect when they arrive.

c. Is the task time sensitive?
  o You need to create a listing to get an FNSKU code. If you want the code labels applied by your supplier then you will need to create a listing by a set time for your supplier.
  o Your initial listing doesn't have to be perfect so you can create a listing just to get the code and then update (refine) the listing later. This means that although the task is time sensitive you can reduce the amount of work required in that timeframe.
  o You will need your images by the time you make your listing live so if you have too many other time commitments you may have to pay for image related tasks (even if you have the skill set yourself).

d. Can you afford to pay for this task to be outsourced?
  o The reason I look at the financial cost of an activity after defining its importance is because no matter how large your budget you should avoid wasting money on excessive activities.

5. Outsourcing tips for beginners
• Be meticulously detailed in the scope of the works that you instruct your VA to undertake.
• Set (and agree) milestones for you to check the progress and quality of the work throughout the process.
• Ask your networks for referrals of VAs they have used.
• Start new VAs with simple tasks and build the complexity as they prove themselves.

6. Where do you outsource to?

a. Firstly we'll assume that you are using Fulfilled By Amazon (for distribution) so you have outsourced the following activities to them:

- Shipping from the intermediary warehouse to Amazon's warehouse. Although you will create the shipping labels (using your Amazon Seller account) you are using Amazon's shipping rates to UPS the cartons so we'll class this as their work.
- Storage of your products ready to ship to customers.
- Hosting of your product listing on their website.
- Use of their online shopping basket to accept customer orders.
- Processing and shipping your product to the customers.
- Providing customer service support (for refunds and returns).
- Sales tax collection.

b. Let's look at the type of activities that you may outsource as part of this business model:

- Product Research
  o Although you will want to undertake product research for your first product it can be very time consuming.
  o As your business grows you may decide to outsource some product research activities, with a detailed criteria you could contract overseas VA's to undertake this.
  o You may find research VAs on Fiverr, Upwork etc. who are capable of this.
- Logo/Packaging Design

- o When it comes to logos and branding you could get something basic from Fiverr or Upwork.
- o For design of your packaging don't be afraid to ask your supplier what other customers have used (to give you a starting point).
- Product Listing script and setup
  - o There are lots of copyrighters out there on sites such as Fiverr and Upwork but ensure you check their bio to ensure they are experienced in Amazon listings (and HTML).
- Image photography
  - o The cost of a professional photographer can be surprisingly reasonable if you shop around in your local area.
- Image editing
  - o If you have outsourced your pictures to a professional you could also pay them to edit them.
  - o A VA could be better suited (and more cost effective) for editing as they may be more experienced with the specifications of Amazon. Check Upwork or Fiverr.
- Factory Inspection
  - o Unless you live in China or want to visit just to check your production it is worth contracting an inspection company to visit the factory (around the 80% production point).
  - o Companies such as V Trust can be contracted to carry out an independent inspection for you and provide you a detailed report of the inspection.
  - o If you are outsourcing an inspection ensure that you provide a detailed scope with the specific things that you want checked.
- Customs Clearance and Repackaging

- o If you live in the USA you can probably handle a fᵢ phone calls to customs and may have the space to repackage your stock (before sending to Amazon).
  - o Once your business expands (and especially if you live overseas) you may want to outsource the receipt and repackaging of your stock from overseas.
  - o Companies like FBA inspections and GDW provide various services including inspections and repackaging (with a variety of services you can determine which, if any are within your budget).
- Sales Tax registration and returns
  - o If you live in the USA you probably have an accountant who can register and prepare your returns for each of the relevant states (hence you are outsourcing to them).
  - o If you are an overseas seller or do not have an accountant you may want to outsource these tasks to a sales tax specialist such as Piesner Johnson.
- The running of your Amazon Business whilst you are on holiday
  - o Assuming at some stage you want to take a break from the everyday grind of checking your listings, you may decide to trust a family member or outsource the everyday running of your listing to a business colleague.
  - o Although you may see your business as your baby you are going to need a babysitter at some stage (but with such an emotional subject I leave your choice of outsourcer to you).

CASE STUDIES

A. Elsa's Amazon Listing

- Elsa determined that of all the tasks she needed to carry out, compiling her listing would be best to outsource.
- She found a VA on Fiverr who lists Amazon listing compilation in his Bio.
- She gave him limited access to her account and he created her listing (using "Merchantwords" to determine the keywords to use).
- Elsa is a part time photographer and so she provided the VA the images to add to the listing.
- Once the listing was live she removed the VAs access to her Amazon account.

B. Grahams' Logo and Packaging

- Graham determined that of all the tasks he needed to carry out his private label logo and packaging would be best to outsource.
- He searched for a VA on Upwork and found two potential candidates.
- He provided them both with the same (detailed) brief as to the type of products and the sizes of logo required.
- Once the VAs fulfilled their assignments he posted both options in his Facebook group and asked the group members to provide feedback on their preferences.
- The designs that got the most votes were sent to the supplier to be used for the product.

C. Fred's Photos

- Fred determined that of all the tasks he needed to carry out his product images would be best to outsource.

- He searched his local area for a Professional Photographer and found a lady (on the internet) who had experience taking product images for magazines.
- Once the images were completed Fred forwarded the images to a VA off Upwork (who was recommended to him by a member of his Facebook group).
- The VA minimized any white spaces on the images and optimized them for Amazon listings.
- Once the VA returned the images to Fred he uploaded them to his listing.

D. Hugo's repackaging

- Hugo repacks his first 1000 units (of his first product) in his garage.
- By the time he has 10 separate products selling on Amazon it makes more sense to outsource this repackaging (to an intermediary) as he should have enough margin factored into these products to pay for it from the sales.
- Hugo contracts a company called FBA Inspections and has his Chinese supplier ship the products directly to their warehouse.
- FBA Inspections checks all the stock and repacks into cartons of 150 (the maximum units per carton that Amazon will accept).
- When the cartons are ready to ship FBA Inspections provide Hugo with the shipment details so that he can create shipping labels from his Amazon Seller account.
- Hugo emails the shipping labels to FBA Inspections (in pdf format) and they organize UPS to collect them from their warehouse and ship to Amazon.

EXERCISE SEVEN COMPILE AND CATEGORIZE A LIST OF ACTIVITIES

The activities needed to get you from your current status to the stage where your product is available for sale on Amazon (feel free to use the timelines exercise in chapter five to help you with this list).

1. Once you have completed your activities list categorize it into which activities you are going to outsource and which activities you are going to undertake yourself.

2. Start investigating sources for the activities that you have decided to outsource.

CHAPTER 7 FINDING THE RIGHT PRODUCT

The term "product research" here refers to researching products to purchase and list on Amazon, starting with a large list and reducing it down to a shortlist of products.

When you talk about product research with an Amazon business builder it can invoke a multitude of emotions from excitement to dread.

Whatever those emotions, the product research and selection part of the process is very important and can determine whether you have a success or a failure in this business.

Although some businesses outsource the initial research to virtual assistants, it is important that you understand the principles and define your search criteria before you go down that line.

1. There are three basic steps to product research

Step 1:   An initial search for ideas and products

Step 2:   Populating a list of potential products

Step 3:   Narrowing down your list using a more detailed
        criteria

2. Step 1:   The initial search

There are lots of sources out there such as social networks (e.g. Instagram, Pinterest and Reddit) that will give you a glimpse into the newest 'in thing' to the market but if you remember, right at the start of the book I said that you are tapping into a market that is already there.

Various sources (such as blogs or other books on the subject of Amazon businesses) recommend not looking at the top 100, 200, 300 or 500 selling products on Amazon for your product selection.

Although using outside sources for inspiration is a great idea, when you are first setting out on this journey you will want products that are already selling on the Amazon platform.

You need to take into account that unless you are adding a product with a view to creating a new market (which can be very expensive in any area) you will be competing against current sellers so you need to ensure that your product is already selling on Amazon.

Competition is not a bad thing as if other sellers have trail blazed and created the market then as long as the market is big enough you should tap into that market.

There is an old adage that if there are twenty of the same shop (e.g. shoe shops) in a street, and there is enough market, ten shops will fail and ten will flourish. Using that analogy you only have to perform better than half of your competition to succeed.

Do you need to use a product you are selling?

a) When I started my initial product research I wasn't metho
and was just looking at products I liked or wanted to purchase
myself. The issues with that were:

- I was living in New Zealand and the market there is a lot
different to America.

- I was a single guy with no children and that demographic
could have discounted couples, people with children, females
etc. who were also purchasing on Amazon.

b) Don't discount an item just because you don't use it (although
it can be an advantage in your initial analysis).

- You may not have pets but pet owners are a large
demographic in America which translates to a large market for
pet products.

- You may choose to stay away from vibrators and other sex
toys (I include this only as an example that there may be
products out there that you haven't even thought about) but
the final decision is yours and should be based on analysis
rather than focusing on just kitchen utensils etc.

Your initial search is about building a mind-set of the kind of
products that you should focus on (and the ones you should
discount).

The more times that you work through this process the more the
criteria will become second nature.

c) Selection criteria is one of the easiest ways to narrow down your product search. Most sellers will use similar criteria but I have distilled below some tips from various sources (to help with your initial research):

- Do not select heavy products.

Shipping heavy objects can severely eat into your margins and in some cases mean no profit at all.

On your initial orders if you are ordering from China you will probably ship your products by Air and this is where weight is very important.

Some people class light as less than two pounds and some people class it as less than a pound in weight (obviously the lighter the better).

- Do not select Trademarked products

Some Chinese suppliers may unintentionally or intentionally reproduce products that are trademarked.

Although they may not intend to get you in trouble you as the seller would be liable (you don't want to be sued by the likes of The Disney corporation) or be stuck with a pile of stock that you can't even liquidate.

- Do not select electronics products or any items that need batteries

Even if you get a percentage of your stock inspected at the facto, the fact is that you have the potential for more defects. I have seen several flashing dog collars and running arm bands that didn't work when they were first opened or failed within 10 minutes.

If a product contains a battery you may have the added problem of shipping restrictions (either needing the batteries shipped separately) or issues due to the chemicals in the battery being classified hazardous.

- Avoid selecting any category where the lead sellers in the category are recognized as a national brand e.g. Coca Cola, Sony, Nikon, Apple.

Large companies invest millions of dollars in building their brand and brand recognition, and when you are initially setting out on this journey I doubt you have the same budget.

Traditionally these products are more expensive so customers tend to be more selective and as such you may have to risk a lot more of your stake money just to get into these areas.

- Ideally select a product where the average sales price is approx. $15-$50.

It has been suggested that once customers look at buying products over $50 they will do more due diligence and this can stop potential opportune purchases.

I personally see the sweet spot as around $20-$25 as most people are prepared to risk this amount on a purchase without too much hesitation. This is also a price that promotes manageable margins and stock (financial) outlay.

- Look for products listing in the top twenty of a particular sub category

Be aware that the higher the number the lower the ranking (e.g. a product ranked 24,000 in a category is ranked lower than a product ranked 100 in the same category) just as an item ranked number ten is lower than an item ranked number one in someone's top ten list.

The assumption here is that based on Amazons algorithm it gives a higher ranking to products that are selling more units (e.g. a product ranked 1000 in a category may sell 25 units a day and a product ranked 8,000 in the same category may only sell 5 units a day).

- Look for products smaller than a 10 inch cube

Ideally look for something smaller than a standard coke can when shipped.

As with heavy items, large items can have expensive shipping costs from China that can severely eat into profit margins.

Large products can also have increased storage costs for Amazon warehouses further eating into profit margins.

- Does the item you are considering have the potential of several purchases?

If your product has the potential to be given as a gift, buyers m purchase more than one item.

If your product is consumable (e.g. aromatherapy oils) your customer will need to buy it again when they have used it.

- Avoid choosing a product that is classed as a commodity

You do not want to choose a product like toilet rolls that can be bought at Walmart (it may also sell on Amazon but probably by someone with deeper pockets than you).

- Avoid fragile items (or items containing liquids).

A crystal glass set may make a nice gift for a buyer but the chances of damage through shipping are high and this can result in returns (and bad reviews).
If you sell an item containing liquids and the customer makes multiple purchases together any leakage from your product could damage their other purchases (leading to more unhappy customers).

3. Step 2: Starting your list

You can start your initial list at the same time as step 1 but I would advise you to have your primary criteria determined before you go out and start a frenzied/directionless search.

You are trying to find 100 -150 items here and the more detailed analysis can be done once you have this number of items.

A. There are three basic steps to creating your initial list:

1. Go an Amazon.com and find the product

2. Go on Alibaba.com and find the identical item (a lot of Amazon sellers use the suppliers pictures so finding the identical product can be easy).

3. Input the details into a table/spreadsheet (I sometimes list the ASIN from Amazon to find it easier to find the item on Amazon later).

B. Starting with a large product list is beneficial in so many ways:

- It is time efficient because once you get into the groove you will find it easier.

- Once you start detailed analysis on the list it will start shrinking and a bigger list at the start will save you having to constantly restart the list building.

C. Be methodical in your product research

- Before I looked at any courses or read any books on the process I chose to track my product research on an Excel spreadsheet.

- If you aren't very IT literate (and you can't work in a basic spreadsheet) you may want to upskill a little before you go any further.

- If you choose a methodical approach it will save you a lot of time later on in avoiding duplication of effort. You will have data showing your previous searches and this can also give you direction for future products.

- I created a simple spreadsheet for tracking my product searches but there are prepopulated spreadsheets out there in the market for just this purpose.

- I highly recommend the spreadsheet provided by the Startup Bros Will Mitchell and Kyle Eschenroeder. I have discussed the Startup Bros elsewhere in the book and (at the time of writing this book) they provide a free spreadsheet on their site to help with the initial analysis plus a 5 hour video which gives a demonstration on use of their spreadsheet

D. Product Categories

I. Here are some of my suggested popular categories (none restricted) to start with:

- Pet Supplies because :
  - o We all love our pets
  - o They can be high maintenance
- Home and Kitchen because
  - o We all need eat
  - o We all need to live somewhere
- Sports because:
  - o We are all trying to live healthier lives
- Health and Personal Care because :
  - o We are vain
  - o We are all getting older and want to have quality of life (an older population requires more maintenance)
  - o There are lots of consumables in this category
- Baby because:
  - o Everyone wants to buy presents for the baby
  - o We all start as babies

II.   I highly advise you not to choose products in a restricted category for your first product. The list below is accurate at the time of writing but as the Amazon system can change at any time ensure you check how up to date this info remains. Categories and products requiring approval:

- Automotive and Powersports
- 2015 Holiday Selling Guidelines in Toys and Games
- Jewellery
- Beauty category: Requirements and application
- Amazon Custom
- Health and Personal Care
- Watches
- Clothing and Accessories
- Video, DVD, and Blu-ray
- Shoes, Handbags and Sunglasses
- Luggage and Travel Accessories
- Carrier-Branded Locked Cell Phones
- Sports Collectibles
- Cell Phone and Accessories
- Collectible Books
- Collectible Coins
- Entertainment Collectibles
- Fine Art
- Gift Cards
- Grocery and Gourmet Foods
- Major Appliances
- Services
- Sexual Wellness
- Wine

III.   If you do choose to sell in a restricted category you will end up experiencing the joys of getting clearance to sell in that category:

- There are certain hoops you have to jump through to be able to sell in a restricted category (also known as ungating). This process can be changed by Amazon at any stage!
- When I got ungated in 'health and personal care', I had to supply 3 receipts each for 5 toothbrushes or some other health and personal care products even though I had invoices from my supplier for hundreds of units of a totally different product.
- Apparently at that stage the receipts from Walmart had their item codes in a specific format that the Amazon system accepted.
- You will see various companies out there that offer to get you ungated in a category and if you decide to sell in one of the restricted categories for one of your future products (I have listed some in the resources category) it is well worth consulting them.

4. Step 3:   Narrowing down your list

Once you have your list (hopefully of 75-150 products) you are going to drill down into another level of research.

A. There are some who suggest basing the product choice on the product ranking in a specific category:

- There are various categories and sub categories so choose wisely.

- The daily ranking can vary widely as it is based on an algorithm that can vary with regard to number of reviews, standard of reviews, number of sales and various other things (such as when a product initially lists).
- If you are using a products ranking as one of your criteria I would suggest tracking the product and its competitors for a week to see if there are any anomalies (don't just accept one day's data).

B. Below is a list of some of the more detailed criteria people use (and you should consider) to choose their products:

- Look for items with 200 - 500 reviews

When a product first launches it may not have many reviews but has a higher price than its competitors, so check the number and date of reviews to ensure the product has been selling for a reasonable period.

Sometimes the initial launch price is just to test the water and is quickly brought down to the level of the product's competitors.

- Search for items that are already selling (e.g. top 100 selling items in each category).

These products may have been selling for a while to get to their current ranking, and that's fine as it shows the product has potential longevity.

To estimate how long a product has been selling look at the dates of the oldest reviews (this should at least provide a ball park figure).

- How can you improve on the product?

Lousy pictures for a product can affect sales so better pictures on your listing can give customers a better experience.

Some individuals will just buy a mass produced ebook to add to a product. This may give it the appearance of added value but if the book isn't really added value you are disrespecting your customers.

- Remember your purpose is not just to find a product that makes money but also a product that adds value to your customers.

Look at the negative reviews for similar / competitors' products.

Look for commonalities and try and filter out genuine issues (with the review process open to abuse sometimes competitors will post nefarious reviews on each other's listings).

When you find genuine issues ask your suppliers how they can address these issues (e.g. if there is a kitchen product with a sharp handle then ask your supplier to produce a product that doesn't have a sharp handle).

C. Profit Calculation

To assist you with estimating the profit from your product you can use the Amazon FBA revenue calculator.

This is a free tool provided by Amazon (in Seller Central) to help you determine the profit on an item if you decide to distribute though FBA. Here's how to use it:

- Login to the FBA calculator

- Choose the product that you are looking at selling on Amazon (you are clicking on the listing of a competitor here to get the data for the calculator).

- Copy the ASIN for the product and paste it into the calculator search box and hit search.

- You will now see two columns

    o The first column entitled "Your fulfilment" is where you can fill in all of the costs should you be distributing your product yourself.

    o The second column entitled "Amazon fulfilment" is where we will focus and fill in the details.

- Type in the price of the item in the listing into the "Start Price" box (we are looking to match the competitor here), let's say this item is $20.00.

- In the inbound shipping we'll simplify here at around $0.50 a pound (as the shipping rates to Amazon within the USA are Amazon's preferred rates).

- We'll assume your product weighs two pounds here so input $1.00

- In the prep service we'll assume you are getting your products prepped by an intermediary (for $0.45 a unit) so we'll put $0.45 here.

- Hit calculate and the table will populate with all the data including Amazon's costs.

- The bottom figure labelled "margin impact" is the amount per unit Amazon should pay you for each unit you sell at the price you put into the Start Price box (based on the figures you input and Amazon's current fee structure.

If you are selling an item for $20.00 on Amazon and the margin impact figure is $14.50 you need to take off the cost of your item to work out your profit (not including tax).

If you paid $4.50 a unit and are selling for $20.00 a unit through FBA and Amazon is paying $14.50 per unit into your account your profit is $10.00 ($14.50- $4.50) per unit.

Although this is only a rough calculation you can see that with Amazon taking around 25% of your sales price you will require reasonable margins to make the business worthwhile.

D. In your initial search you got the price on Amazon and the price for the same item on Alibaba, you now need to consider these extra costs:

- Shipping

You can roughly estimate the cost of shipping using the freight calculator at worldfreightrates.com (or various other tools out there).

Assuming that your first shipment will be (small enough to) be shipped via air you will need the following information for the calculator:

- Origin Airport (pick the closest to your supplier).
- Destination Airport (pick the closest to you).
- The Commodity type (this will probably be "General Merchandise").
- Commodity value (this will be the cost of your goods from the supplier).
- The Gross weight, height, width and length of a carton.
- If you are unsure of any of the dimensions check Alibaba and if not shown on a listing ask the supplier.
- Ensure you tick the box marked insurance and press the button marked "Get Rate".
- You will now have a rough rate per carton and depending on the number of units in each carton you will have to multiply the figure from the calculator by the number of cartons to get your shipment total (e.g. if your first shipment will be 1000 units and they only ship ten units per carton you have to multiply the figure that the freight calculator provided by 100).
- Although your supplier may be able to get a slight reduction on shipping this calculator can quickly show which products will be so costly to ship that there is not enough margin to make the product profitable.

- Import duty costs

Although your shipment may be too small to merit customs fees it is always worth being prepared to factor in extra costs.

The website dutycalculator.com provides a calculator that provides a percentage for duty rate calculation.

This paid calculator allows two or three free calculations (at the time of writing) and you then have to wait 24 hours before you get any further free calculations or pay.

By estimating shipping costs first you will have the required details for the duty calculator.

- Inspection costs

Most of the inspection companies charge a daily rate (currently approximately USD$300) to inspect your products at the factory.

Depending on the factory location or the complexity of the inspection you may pay more so check with your inspection company for their current rates.

- Repackaging / processing costs

Although intermediaries tend to provide a multitude of services the basic repackaging will usually cost $0.45- $0.50 a unit so feel free to add that cost into your considerations

5. Product Research Tools

ere are lots of free products and software tools out there to help with understanding potential sales but here I am just going to cover a couple of software tools to help with product research.

A. Jungle Scout (also known as JS – can be purchased from JungleScout.com) is the first tool we will discuss.

- This is a paid Google Chrome extension.

- Although Amazon do not make their sales data available to external sources the use of Jungle Scout provides a rough guide that can help you with more detailed drilling down from your large product list.

- Once you have downloaded Jungle Scout you will see a "JS" icon in the top right hand corner of your screen (when logged on to Google Chrome).

- If you carry out a product search on your Amazon page using the Google chrome browser, you can now create a table (with JS) that provides product information including the sales ranking, estimated sales, estimated sales revenue and number of reviews etc.

- This table can be exported to a spreadsheet as well to allow you more detailed research.

- There are more and more similar tools coming onto the market and as individuals tend to have preferences in the way they like tools to perform feel free to visit their site and play with their free resources first.

- This is not a sales pitch for Jungle scout and the author is not promoting the product but I have used it to some success.

B. Terapeak is a product that is useful for determining the amount of competition for a product

- Although Amazon do not make their sales data available to external sources Terapeak utilizes the data from EBay and provides one of the closest things to Amazon data that can help you with more detailed drilling down from your large product list.

- EBay is not exactly the same as Amazon but as it is one of the only nationwide online sellers in America that provides detailed sales data it is one of the best options.

- Terapeak uses the EBay data to allow you to analyse a product and determine if your product is selling and if enough market still exists for your product (not too many sellers).

- Although the EBay data is the closest you will get to actual Amazon data, EBay and Amazon are two different animals.

- The info from Terapeak (like so many other resources) is just a guide and once you have completed your analysis only you can decide if you are willing to take a risk on a product.

- There are more and more similar tools coming onto the market and as individuals tend to have preferences in the way they like tools to perform feel free to visit their site and subscribe for their 7 day free trial.

- I would suggest that you don't start the trial until you are ready to begin your more intensive product research (as your 7 day trial might be enough to choose your first products).

- This is not a sales pitch for Terapeak and the author is not promoting the product but I have used it to some success.

CASE STUDIES

1. David decided to focus on Pet Supplies

- He has populated his spreadsheet with 113 items that all have a price ratio of 3:1 or more (e.g. if he bought them at the listed price of $5 on Alibaba he would need to sell for the $20 listed price on Amazon).

- The 3:1 ratio is a rough benchmark that allows some wiggle room for marketing costs etc. and provides an initial tool to reduce the rough research list.

- Using Jungle Scout he narrows his list down to 10 items.

- He assumes a product below a category ranking of 1500 will not provide enough sales.

- He determines that the best potential product is a set of doggy nail clippers.

- The top 3 competitor listings are ranked 665, 782 and 853 in the pet supplies category.

- The Clippers are selling for approx. $20.00 on Amazon and are listed on Alibaba at approx. $2.10 a unit (based on an MOQ of 1000 units).

- David determines the number of units per carton that the supplier uses for shipping and the other dimensions of the cartons (this information is all available on the Alibaba listing without David having to contact the potential supplier).

- He uses the carton details to estimate the shipping (to be $250 per carton) via the calculator on worldfreightrates.com.

The 1000 units would ship in 5 cartons of 200 units so he multiplies his findings by 5 to settle on a total of $1250 for shipping (approx. $1.25 a unit to ship 1000 units.

- Using the duty calculator he estimates that the duty rate at 7% of $2100 (the cost of 1000 units at $2.10) is $147.

- His initial estimates for his product are now $3.50 a unit (based on $2.10 supply + $1.25 shipping + $0.15 duty).

- This rough cost is well within the $5.00 budget and so he decides to proceed with contacting suppliers for quotes.

2. Amelia decided to focus on kitchen items

- She has populated her spreadsheet with 127 items.

- After comparison of the products through Terapeak she narrows her products down to 5 items.

- In more detailed research she finds the best product (item with the best margins after including shipping and duty) was a coffee grinder.

- Her initial estimate is that the grinder sells for $22.00 a unit and will cost her $4.00 a unit to have sitting in Amazon's warehouses.

- Based on these rough estimates she determines it is worth pursuing the grinder further and decides to contact suppliers.

EXERCISE EIGHT START YOUR PRODUCT RESEARCH

1. Create a list of at least 100 products that you believe meet your criteria.

2. Narrow that list down to three products with the best potential (and profit margins).

3. Determine which of your chosen products you will contact suppliers for quotes

- Don't be afraid to have real time chats (with suppliers) to gather the information in estimating shipping rates etc.

- If you do start chatting at these early stages be professional and leave yourself an out (telling a supplier you need to get permission to make a decision is not a sign of weakness and allows you the chance to contact them again for further information).

Summary

You have been estimating your costs and calculations on the product prices (and MOQs) listed on alibaba.com.

You should now have a shortlist of products ranging from 3-10 products

Assuming that you have estimated most of your costs to get the product from a factory in China to Amazon's warehouse and that there is still enough profit margin in your product you now need detailed costings.

In the next chapter we will focus on your dealings with suppliers and helping you find one.

CHAPTER 8 FINDING A SUPPLIER

Once you have found a product that meets your initial criteria you then need to find a company to supply you that product.

Although you may be using suppliers in different countries (including USA) I'm primarily going to focus on China in this chapter.

a) Before you start contacting Suppliers on Alibaba set up a separate email address

If you have set up a business/website and have a business email you can use this but I highly recommend not using your personal email.

Even if you don't have a business yet you will usually find a gmail account available that suits (e.g. if you are calling your business Kitchen Stuff you can probably open an account with Kitchenstuff@gmail.com or Kitchenstuff1@gmail.com).

The sellers on Alibaba tend to send you lots of emails (you may think of it as spam but to them it's just marketing).

b) Initial Supplier Search

Initially whilst you are looking through the suppliers (for your designated product) you may find the same product with a variety of prices:

- Some suppliers will list a price range (e.g. $0.50 - $2.50) and an MOQ (Minimum Order Quantity). This usually means that the MOQ (e.g. 1000) is not just the smallest quantity that you can order but that the highest price is the price that you will pay for that minimum quantity.

- The price from a price range tend to reduce towards the lower price the more units you order.

- Some suppliers on Alibaba list outrageous prices (in comparison to other suppliers of the same product). This could mean that they have fantastic quality in comparison to their competitors but usually means that they have just thrown a price up there (and are unsure of the true pricing of the product) and want you to contact them.

- If there is only one supplier for a product with multiple listings don't be surprised if the first quote you receive is nothing like the price quoted on Alibaba (treat this as a starting point for negotiations).

c) Initial Supplier Contact

Your initial contact (with a supplier) will usually be via the "Chat Now" or "Contact Supplier" button on Alibaba.com.

- It is worth having a template (I have mine in a word doc) that you cut, doctor and paste into the chat.

- My chat includes various pieces of information to save me repeating them constantly e.g:

  o I am a sourcer for a company looking to add more products to our current product lines.

  o My initial bulk order will be 500-1000 units and once we have established a permanent supply chain it is anticipated orders will increase to 1000-5000 units a month.

- o I want suppliers that accept PayPal and Alibaba Trade Assurance.

- o I expect a turnaround of a maximum 20 days from order placement to shipping (of orders up to 2000 units).

d) The pros and cons of multiple samples

You may find that when you first start out you want to get moving fast and order multiple samples.

Pros:

Of course this might mean that your initial cash outlay will be larger but potentially you could be launching multiple products at once (or in a row).

There are companies you can use to bundle the samples together in China (this can reduce your shipping costs).

Cons:

The downside here is that if you are just starting out you may make all of your mistakes on multiple products at once and this can increase your risk.

Financially if you are outlaying your funds on multiple products (as samples and then larger orders) you could decimate your budget in a very short period.

e) Ordering your first samples

Your initial contact with suppliers may be via instant message on Alibaba:

Don't be afraid to ask questions about size and number of units per carton etc.

Before you order the samples you want to know how much the bulk order will be per unit so check that before ordering samples.

Most suppliers will not charge you for samples but will expect you to pay the shipping

- Expect the initial shipping may be $100 or more, don't haggle too hard here as they will not think you are serious.

- The cost of samples can come as a shock to first time shoppers but this is just one of the facts of the process.

- When you order your initial samples you may end up just paying via credit card or PayPal (if you are only risking $100 you want to get the samples as quick as possible).

f) Paying your Supplier

- You may assume that if your supplier is classed as a Gold Supplier (on Alibaba) that nothing can go wrong but in order to reduce the risk you need to determine how you are going to pay your supplier:

- PayPal – (Paying through your PayPal account on PayPal.com).

  There are several benefits of a purchase using PayPal:

    o You are afforded some purchase protection. If there is an issue with your purchase you can raise a dispute within 45 days of purchase date and PayPal will work on your behalf until the issue is resolved.

    o The funds are deposited straight into the supplier's PayPal account (and they can transfer them straight into their bank account) so they can start production without delay.

There are some restrictions on that buyer protection:

- Purchasing a Privately Labelled (PL) product can negate some of your protections so don't assume that just using PayPal is some kind of Golden insurance

- If you are paying in instalments (e.g. 50% pre-production and the rest once the production run is complete) this can also negate the buyer protection.

How the Purchase protection tends to work:

- The protection covers you for non-delivery or delivery of Items significantly not as described (remember the caveats on PL items etc.).

- If you open a dispute on your account PayPal allow 20 days to resolve this.

- If you open a claim immediately (or the resolution can't be achieved on a dispute within the 20 days) the supplier has 10 days to reply to the claim.

- If the supplier replies within the 10 days PayPal work to resolve the claim but that can take 30 days plus.

- Although these time frames are open to change be aware this can be a lengthy process if you need the funds to make a purchase to replace the order that has gone amiss.

Not all suppliers will accept payment via PayPal

The use of PayPal also comes with a financial cost.

- o If you have previously purchased single items online (e.g. an eBook or an electrical item) using PayPal, the supplier probably absorbed the fees and they weren't apparent to you.

- o When you are making a commercial purchase most suppliers will expect you to pay the additional fees for the convenience of paying via PayPal.

- o PayPal fees usually sit at around 5% and although your supplier may agree to split this fee this may be an extra cost in your budget that you need to bear in mind.

- TRADE ASSURANCE (a free payment protection service form Alibaba.com)

Alibaba Trade assurance
https://www.youtube.com/watch?v=XJl3wa0K84s

The benefits of a purchase using Alibaba's trade assurance is that you are afforded some purchase protection.

In this situation you ensure that your supplier is part of the scheme (this will be apparent on Alibaba.com) and ensure the amount that they are covered for covers the cost of your purchase. Just as you wouldn't insure your $30,000 car for $10,000 you wouldn't want to place an order with your supplier for $30,000 if they were only covered for $10,000.

You must hire an inspector (as per the contract).

If the product is not as per the contract or there are delays in production Alibaba refund you the money.

When ordering using Trade Assurance you need to keep a close eye on your timetable:

- o If the supplier had 30 days to make the product and isn't going to hit the target you need to agree to an amendment of the Trade assurance period.

- o The payment from Alibaba can take 30 days or so from the dispute being resolved. Although these time frames are open to change be aware this can be a lengthy process if you need the funds to make a purchase to replace the order that has gone amiss.

As you are paying the money to Alibaba and they are then paying the supplier this can cause a day or so delay in production (which is something to take into account if you are working to a tight deadline).

A lot of first time buyers do a lot of communication with suppliers via email. In order to benefit from Trade Assurance you need to utilize Alibaba.com:

- o You need to ensure that you use the Trade Assurance to communicate with your supplier and for placing your order (so that Alibaba.com can track this).

- o This also allows you to have your service agreement and terms trackable by Alibaba.com

- o You and your supplier need to complete these terms. Ensure you confirm the contract in the Trade Assurance before moving on to payment.

- o You must make your payment to the Citibank account (that alibaba.com have allocated for your supplier) and not any other account to ensure you are covered by Trade assurance

- WIRE TRANSFER – (Usually depositing the money directly into a supplier's bank account).

Some suppliers will not accept PayPal or work through the Trade Assurance option.

Although some Amazon businesses are happier to purchase using wire transfer when you are first starting out I would advise against this.

You need to realize that the risks involved in Wire transfer here are much higher than PayPal or Trade Assurance.

You have little or no protections on your payment and all I will say here is "BUYER BEWARE".

g) Test your Samples thoroughly

- If you purchase items with built in batteries (e.g. a LED Dog collar) leave them on for a constant period as this can help determine:

  o How long does the battery last?

  o Are there any issues with the unit being left on for extended periods (overheating etc.)?

- Sell some samples on EBay (or your local equivalent to get feedback from real customers).

h) Using an independent examination company in China

Although paying for an independent inspection company may seem excessive on your first shipment (especially if your first shipment is only costing $1200-$1500 and an inspector can be an extra $300) this sets the tone with a new supplier and can save you a lot more money further on in the process.

If you are paying via trade assurance you will need to pay an inspection company as per the contract.

When you order your first bulk order from an overseas supplier it is highly recommended that you pay an inspection company. By getting the product inspected before it leaves the factory it can avoid costs in time and money.

Time - If you get the inspection done early enough it can reduce any delays in production due to remanufacturing.

Money - If you wait until your product arrives in the US and there are issues it may cost you to send the products back to the supplier or to dispose of the defective products.

If you do hire an inspection company you need to determine what you want to be inspected.

- Firstly you want to make sure that the product is the same as your samples:
    - Colour
    - Size
    - Material
    - Weight

- Next you want to ensure that the shipping requirements have been met:
    - Number of units per carton
    - Size of carton
    - Weight of carton

- Although you should have addressed potential issues when you ordered your samples you want to make sure that your product is the best quality (and hopefully exceeds your competition).

  Check out the negative reviews on your competitors' listings and see if there is anything that you can check before shipping:

    o If your competitors has a product that breaks easily, get your inspectors to try and break one unit (ensure you tell the supplier you will pay for the extra unit).

    o If your competitors' product has an offensive smell get that checked out.

    o By reducing potential issues in your product manufacture it can address two issues:

        1. Reduce the number of negative reviews you should receive on your listings.

        2. Make you the more confident if there are nefarious reviews posted on your listing (competitors have been known to do this).

i) Placing your first bulk order

- Piggy Backing

  - If you order an identical item to a current seller on Amazon you can piggy back off their listing (add your products to someone else's listing and images).

- The problem with piggybacking is that if you are selling the same product as your competition the only differentiation may be price and it can become a cost cutting race (to see who can sell the cheapest).

- Private Labelling

    - Private labelling a product can be as simple as printing/engraving your brand on a product.

    - You can add nicer packaging and add improvements to a product (usually at little extra cost) and in this situation you require your own listing.

j) Are you paying for repackaging etc?

Most Chinese suppliers will pack as many units into a carton as possible but as Amazon (at the time of writing this) only accept a max 150 units per carton, you need to get the stock sent to you or to an intermediary in the USA to repackage the products. Overseas sellers (and even sellers in the States once their business starts to grow in size) will need to contract someone like GDW or FBA inspections for this.

These intermediary companies provide various services from straight forwarding of cartons to repacking and initial inspections.

You may not require all of your units inspected if you have had them inspected in China but it is worth ensuring that the cartons are serviceable as Amazon will not accept damaged cartons into their warehouses.

k) Keeping lines of communication open with sellers

When you initially contact a supplier there are several reasons why you will not continue through to placing a bulk order with them:

- They may have bad communication or no communication.

- The samples they supply may be of a lower quality than their competitors.

- The samples they supply may be more expensive than their competitors.

Dependent on the stage of the process you reach with a supplier you may want to keep communications open.

It is your decision when and how to break off relationships with suppliers and if you choose to just ignore their emails or messages that is up to you but here are a few suggestions to keep the lines of communication open.

i) If the product samples were okay but you have just decided not to pursue that specific product:

- Suggest that you have spoken to your superiors and although you are happy with the product they are not willing to proceed with this product at the moment. You would like to keep in touch and are happy for them to forward similar product ideas later e.g. catalogues.

- Tell them that the time is not currently suitable but could they contact you again in 3 months (etc.).

ii) If the product samples were not up to the required quality so you have decided not to pursue that specific product:

- Suggest that you have spoken to your superiors and currently you have a few issues that need addressing (list the issues specifically). You would like to keep in touch and are happy for them to forward similar product ideas later should the issues be addressed.

Always try to leave the doors open as you never know what a supplier will have available in the future.

iii) Potential teething problems

Your first order is due and you find that your supplier hasn't got the stock (you have paid 50% upfront). Your options:

- Find another supplier, raise a case with Alibaba to recover initial payment (it can take a month or so to recover the funds).

- Give the supplier another chance.

There could have been a genuine issue outside the supplier's control (on one of my orders I was pushing the supplier not knowing their province of China was suffering from 100 year floods).

If you are paying through Trade Assurance (in this case) you need to amend the contract on the platform.

- Drop the product and find another.

It could be that this supplier was the only feasible manufacturer for this particular product.

Whilst you are tied up with this product you are not progressing with other more profitable products so you need to have a walkaway point in mind.

CASE STUDY

Georgina lives in Australia and has decided to venture into the world of selling on Amazon.com

After product research she has narrowed her choice down to a set of ceramic knives

The knives are listed at $2.01-$4.10 MOQ of 2000 by one supplier on Alibaba and $3.00, MOQ of 5000 by another Alibaba seller.

- Georgina contacts both suppliers and tells them that her company are looking to add products to their current range.

- Although the suppliers both had large MOQ's she negotiates a price of $3.50 per unit for an MQ of 1000 (stating that this was based on sample orders and that the order sizes would increase as the year proceeded). The $3.50 includes engraving with the "Cut Once" brand.

- At this stage she has only negotiated prices so the next step is to order samples, she orders ten samples (not engraved to save time) from each supplier, shipped to her in Australia.

- The suppliers charge $70USD each for the samples and they arrive within 5 days of despatch.

- Both sets look identical (and good quality).

- Georgina keeps a set and gets her husband to test a set to destruction (from each supplier), ensuring she marks which set came from which supplier.

- She sells the remaining 16 sets on EBay Australia (to recoup some of her costs and to see if anyone will buy them).

- As both suppliers are so close the deciding factor is the production time. Supplier A needs 22 days for production and Supplier B cannot complete their production in less than 30 days.

- Georgina orders 1000 units from Supplier A and explains to supplier B that her superiors are not willing to wait the extra week but she would like to keep in touch.

- The 1000 Units will be shipped to the USA but she has arranged for an extra 3 units to be dispatched to her in Australia (this way she has Private labelled samples available for image photography.)

- She now has a backup supplier if she ever needs one (a supplier whose quality she has tested).

EXERCISE NINE CONFIRM YOUR FIRST PRODUCT FOR LAUNCH

- Contact at least three suppliers of that product on Alibaba and negotiate the best deal you can for a shipment of 1000 (do not place the order for 1000 units!).

- Order a sample of 10-15 sample units of your chosen product (from at least one supplier).

- If your product will be Private labelled you want to try get sample PLs (especially if you are an overseas buyer).

CHAPTER 9 SETTING UP YOUR LISTING

We will assume by now that you have determined which tasks to outsource and which tasks to undertake yourself (See the section on what to do and what to outsource earlier).

A. When setting up your listing the text is broken down into three main components:

1. The Title

- There is a balancing act between a title that gives enough information and a title that gives too much:

    o You are allowed approximately 250 characters for most product listings so try to use most of them.

- The keywords that you put into the title are important because:

    o This is the first thing that people see when they read your listing and you want them to be motivated to click on that title.

    o When customers are searching for your product (or similar products) in a search the snapshot of your listing that Amazon displays can be very small. Your Ad needs to catch customers' eyes.

- o The Amazon algorithm and Pay Per Click (PPC) takes these words into account when potential customers type into Amazon to search for products (this determines where your product is displayed on a results page).

- Ensure that when you type the words into your title that you are specific and you have determined they are being searched for:

  - o E.g. If customers are searching for "Ceramic Knife Sets" don't type "Ceramic Knives" in your title.

- Although you might think putting your brand at the start of the Title is a benefit, it is rare that a potential customer will type in your brand name in their initial search (unless you have a huge brand like Coca Cola)

- Yes you want your title to catch buyers' eyes but it is important that your words show up in searches. The use of keywords is a way to optimize the chance of you matching a search.

- A keyword is a word that a potential buyer is typing into the Amazon search box.

- One of the ways to determine the keywords that buyers are using is by subscribing to a service such as merchantwords.com or keywordinspector.com

  - o The basic premise here is that you type in a list of words that you assume your potential customers will type when looking for your product. Merchantwords (or its competitors) will rank these words to show you the words that are being typed in more for searches.

- o You then ensure that your title includes the higher ranking words.

- o E.g. You are listing a Ceramic knife set you may type in words like "Knife Set", "Ceramic Knives", "Rust free knives"

- When typing your listing the tendency can be to use capital letters, commas and bolding etc. but just typing it as you would an MS word type document doesn't mean that it will display as you expect.

- HTML (Hyper Text Markup Language) is a standardized system used to format text when building websites or creating content on the worldwide web.

- Most people have heard of coding (a typed language understood by computers) or HTML but if you have never seen anything like this I advise you to go to any listing on Amazon.com and press the "CTRL" and "U" keys together. A new tab should now open and you can see the source code used for that listing.

- If you are a little competent and want to save some time you can copy and paste some of the code from another Amazon listing if you like a certain effect on that listing (obviously opening the code on that listing with the CTRL,U).

- If you don't feel competent writing your listing (or you are short of time) you can outsource this task to a VA off Fiverr or Upwork etc.

- If you are looking at upskilling there is a website called codeschool.com that provides detailed instructions for most levels.

2. About the Product

- In this section you are selling customers on the benefits of your product's features, your sales pitch.

- As you are limited to 5 bullet points here ensure that each bullet point includes one of your best features and the benefits of that feature:
  - E.g. Individual blade covers included [Feature] reduce the chance of you cutting yourself [Benefit].

- Earlier in this book I suggested that when you are researching your product you take into account the negative reviews of your competitors and ensure your product is improved (to negate those issues).

- Ensure that these improvements are listed in this benefits section.

3. Product Description

- Here you are providing more detailed information on your product.

- You appealed to individuals limited attention span in the five bullet points in section two but if they have read to section three they are clearly interested (known as a hot lead in the sales business), expand on your product.

- If your competitors had questions on your listings you can bet that you will get the same questions so answer the questions in advance in this section (e.g. is this BBQ glove a one size fits all could be pre answered with this glove fits any male with a glove size up to large although not recommended for very small hands

B. Images (Pictures sell so get this right).

Ensure that you use all of the image spaces that Amazon allows you for a listing.

If you have great packaging showcase this in your images (great packaging looks good for gifts).

If you are giving away a free ebook get a graphic of the book cover made up and use that as one of the images (ensure it says EBOOK in big letters as some customers will expect a paper book).

You can swap your pics around later (you may want to add a Christmas tree to the lead picture) for the holidays etc.

If you have a good smartphone (and limited funds) you can take your own pictures but ensure they are good quality and if necessary get a VA to optimize them.

When editing your pics ensure you minimize the white space and that the image meets Amazon's criteria.

C. Initial Pricing of your product

When you input the initial pricing into your listing the "listing price" should be larger than your "sales price" so that it shows discount as you reduce or have sales prices.

In the time that your initial stock was ordered and before you start your listing your competitors may have all dropped their prices.

You do not know the quality of their product so don't be tempted to launch too low.

If you have added value (e.g. a stronger product and an ebook) then launch at your original price and you can always lower prices later.

Although some may advise you that better pictures and a better listing can let you charge a higher price, if you do not have a quality product and your competitors have all dropped their prices you may get lots of early returns (which is not good for your account).

If your product is being sold by competitors and there is a price range of $10- $25 you need to ensure that you still have some margin if your price had to be dropped to the lower price.

Your price needs to take into account Amazon fees as well as your purchase costs (including shipping etc.).

- Although you may need to sell at a certain price just to break even the market does not care about your issues so you should have factored in the pricing when you ordered your stock.
- Remember the difference between a business and a hobby is that the business should put money in your pocket and the hobby may take money out of your pocket. This is a business you are building!
- Always be looking at growing your sales.

D. Categories

You need to determine which category (and sub category) your product is being listed in.

You may decide that your product is going to be a health and personal care product and (once you are cleared to sell in this category) you think your choices are over.

Sub categories can be just as important for your rankings.

Let's look at options for replacement electric toothbrush heads as an example.

Option 1:

- Category   Health and Personal Care
- Sub Category   Oral Care
- Sub-Sub Category   Toothbrushes
- Sub-Sub-Sub Category   Battery Powered Toothbrushes

Option 2:

- Category   Health and Personal Care
- Sub Category   Oral Care
- Sub-Sub Category   Toothbrushes
- Sub-Sub-Sub Category   Electric Toothbrushes

I chose this product as it is easy to see that as you drill down to the relevant sub categories you need to be precise.

With your product you may have a lot more options of categories so please spend some time in choosing which category (and sub categories) you will be listing in.

Check out which sub categories your opposition are mainly listing in and look at matching them.

EXERCISE TEN SET UP A DUMMY LISTING

Setting up your listing may seem daunting but you don't know if you can until you try.

I suggest that you try a listing before you outsource this task.

Ideally pick the item you are going to launch and work through the listing process.

In Seller Central type "List your first item" in the search box.

In the search results you will find "Video Tutorial List your first item". Follow the tutorial and fill in the details for your first product (you can always delete this practice listing later so don't worry that you need to use this to list your first product).

Amazon's Seller Central section provides an abundance of tutorial videos covering their processes (including how to set up a listing).

I suggest looking in Seller Central first as Amazon update their videos whenever they change their processes (and they're free).

CHAPTER 10 DESIGN AND MARKETING

You may have the best product in the world but if it looks like a toilet roll wrapped in newspaper it will rarely sell.

Even if you have a great looking product you still need to market it. I like to use the analogy that if you built a great railway station and didn't have tracks going to the station you would get no trains. If no one knows about your product how (or why) would they buy it?

A. Product launch marketing steps.
    1. Create listing

        a) This has been covered in the previous chapter

    2. Set up a feedback system ('feedback genius', 'feedback 5', 'Salesbacker' etc.)

        a) One of the most common ways to interact with your customers is through a feedback system such as (Seller Labs) feedback genius.
        b) Here you can link software directly to your Amazon seller account and automatically send out emails to your customers when they purchase.
        c) Some of the benefits of using a system like this are:
            • This provides automated customer support that can foster good relations with your customers
            • You can set the system to send a series of emails at set intervals (e.g. on item dispatch, 4 days after dispatch and 10 days after dispatch) which can help solicit positive reviews and can also reduce bad reviews as the customer can contact you here.

- If you are giving away an e-book etc. with your product it can be automatically distributed with the first email after purchase.
- Automation frees up your time and reduces costs of customer support.

3. Create a URL (Uniform Resource Locator)

   a) URL is an acronym that stands for Uniform Resource Locator and is a reference (an address) to a resource on the Internet. When you click on the URL link (in a document etc.) it takes you directly to a specific place on the internet.

   b) When you send someone a URL link in a document or email (or attached to a YouTube video) they can click on that URL and be navigated straight to the place on the internet that the link is paired to.

   c) A Super URL is a link that allows you to choose the path that the internet takes to your Amazon Listing (see the Glossary section for further explanation of the Super URL).

   d) In the next paragraph I'll explain how to create a simple URL.

   e) Remember that keywords in searches are important to the ranking of your product and affect whether or not your product listing is shown to customers when they type in those keywords.

   f) Some people see Super URLs as manipulation of the Amazon system (and a breach of Amazons terms) so I won't describe the process for creating a Super URL.

   g) Whilst I am writing this book there are still guides out there to create Super URLSs (look at AMZtracker.com, and many others).

4. How to create a URL for your listing

   a) Open up the listing page for your product.
   b) Copy and paste all the text in the search box (it should start "www.amazon.com"). Note: this is the search box in Google Chrome, Firefox etc. and not the search box in Amazon.
   c) You may find that these links are a bit long and if you want to turn them into smaller links you can subscribe to sites like tinyurl.com or Bitly.com
   d) When you want to promote your product, copy and paste the relevant link and customers can go straight to your product.

5. Get pre-launch reviews

   a) If you have given away stock before the listing went live those people will not be showing as having purchased your item and so their review will not be marked as a verified purchase.
   b) Individuals can still post reviews on your listing even if they do not have a purchase registered on their account so pre-launch reviews can give you a jump start on your listing.

6. Get your family and friends to review

   a) We all like to support our family's endeavours and so your family may be willing to pay full price for your product (and this will then show as a verified review).
   b) Our families can be quite critical so this drives us to provide a quality product.
   c) Families tend to err on the positive side so these initial reviews should be of a higher star rating.

7. Discount stock for reviews

a) In order to discount stock you need to create discount codes and as this is one of the activities that scares people (worried about losing all of their stock for $0.01 a unit) I have listed a step by step guide in this book's Resources section.

b) Ideally give away 50-150 units (at a discount) at your launch for genuine reviews.

c) Anecdotally, it is said that if you discount your product so that the purchase price is less than $2 Amazon will not mark those reviews as a verified purchase. Even if you charge more they may still not be marked as "verified".

d) Amazon change their terms and the way they do things regularly so by the time you read this book the amount of discount that works for you may vary (either way you need reviews on your listing).

e) There are more and more review groups popping up on Facebook and elsewhere (as people like free products) so if you have a decent product people will happily buy it at a discounted price and give you a genuine review.

f) Don't be tempted to purchase reviews as this is a breach of Amazon's terms and could stop your Amazon business in its tracks.

g) Include an insert with your product that reminds people how to place a review.

h) Ensure that your insert also reminds customers to place seller feedback as this also feeds the Amazon algorithm.

8. Choose your reviewers wisely

    a) You want your reviewers to place an honest review but not all reviewers are equal.
    b) Review Kick and some other review sites let you see the average review that a reviewer gives and lets you select which reviewers to use.
    c) By choosing your reviewers carefully you are not cheating but are trying to avoid being discriminated against.
    d) We all remember a school teacher who marked more harshly or more moderately than the others. Human nature means that no matter how unbiased we try to be we are driven by our life's experiences.
    e) You do not want a reviewer who believes that nobody deserves a 5 star review as future customers will not take into account the reviewer's history.

9. Once you have received some reviews (ideally 50+) start Pay Per Click [PPC]

    a) Don't pay money for PPC until you have positive reviews on your listing as this provides a pedigree for your customers to look at.
    b) PPC is an internal advertising system within the Amazon sales platform which allows your product to be advertised on Amazon depending on the search terms typed by customers.
    c) Pay Per click works an auction system where you are bidding on the key words that customers will search for and if you have the winning bid, Amazon will show your Ad when an Amazon customer types that word in the search box.

d) The higher auction bids usually have their Ads positioned on the "first page" that appears when a customer searches.

e) If a customer scrolls to the next page of search results they are shown ads where Sellers have placed lower bids for the keyword.

f) Customers tend not to scroll too far so the more pages they have to scroll to find your advertisement (ad) the less chance you have of your ads converting to sales.

g) When a prospective customer clicks on your ad you pay a fee.

h) When you set up a PPC campaign you can either manually choose which search words trigger your ad to appear or set up an automatic campaign for Amazon to choose.

- You set a daily budget and an average cost per word (e.g. $10 a day and $0.70 per word).

- Amazon displays an estimated value for each word so if a word is estimated at $0.30 and you set a blanket limit of $0.70, when your ad is shown (due to a person typing in that keyword) you only pay $0.30 if they click on your advertisement.

- When you set up a manual campaign you can set a specific value for each word (e.g. you might set the word "knife" at $0.20 and "knives" at $0.25 in your campaign).

- If your budget per keyword is lower than the estimate on Amazon your ad may not show as often as other advertisers but if their daily budget is used up your ad may show at the lower price.

B. Post Launch Marketing

1. Give away stock on a regular basis

    a) I am not promoting giving away products for false reviews.

    b) Even when you send out reminder emails, buyers rarely provide organic reviews so providing products at a discount for people to review will maintain the number of fresh reviews.

2. Branding

    You are (more than likely) competing with other sellers listing the same item on Amazon. If you want to be competitive you need to own the buy box.

    - The buy box is the box on a products listing page where customers can begin the purchasing process.
    - Because there can be several sellers on Amazon offering the same product for sale, the seller that the customer chooses to buy from is said to own the buy box.

3. Marketing your products

    - FB pages or blogs to create a brand and/or community and then use them to launch products in that line (e.g., kitchens r us is your FB page and when launching kitchen products have a give-away by getting your audience to share your links with their friends
    - Amazon (PPC) Pay Per Click
    - Google ADS

4. Buying images and ensuring you have the appropriate rights

    - Even if you buy images, or you have someone else buy them for you, check that the images have been registered or if free whether acknowledgement/credit is required
    - It is very important that when you are using images in a listing of an e-book that you have the publishing privileges for that image.
    - Some images that seem free on the internet have a caveat (stating 'not to be used for commercial purposes') so be careful.
    - When contracting a V.A. to produce print work (or digital products) confirm that they are using only verified images, or ideally supply your own.

5. Do you need a website

    - For your initial Amazon listing there is no real need for a website but if you want to get brand registry on Amazon you will need a website.
    - If you are going to build a website you need to determine what you want out of it.
        - If you want a site just as a showcase (business card type) for your products that you can edit yourself you may want a Word Press based site.
        - If you want a site primarily as a shop front, a platform such as Shopify may be the best option for you.

- Outsourcing your website build may seem like the obvious option but there are a few things to keep in mind
  - You will need the content ready for a website builder (they don't wave a magic wand and read your mind), compiling this info can be time consuming.
  - If you are not technically minded and your VA builds the site with Weebly, Wix or Word Press you will probably need to pay your VA every time you need a small change or update to your site.
  - As your business grows it may be more cost effective to pay someone to for the upkeep of your site but for convenience (and to avoid frustration) spend a little time learning some basic skills.

CASE STUDY

A. Julie's Review launch

Julie has her listing ready to go and her first product has been received into Amazon's Warehouse (the units should be classed as fulfillable in the next 48hrs).

It is now time to initiate her launch

- Julie creates a URL for her listing.
- As soon as the stock is fulfillable she creates a set of 16 codes for her friends and family.

- Although she has linked feedback software to her seller account (and verified it with test emails) she uses one of the codes herself on her personal Amazon account and confirms everything is working.
- She emails 15 people an individual code and the URL.
- As she ordered her unit using her Amazon Prime Account she receives it within 2 days and confirms the process has gone as planned.
- She now creates another 100 individual codes and gives them to a review group to distribute.
- The reviews from the first 15 discount codes are coming in but it takes another week or so before the second group of reviews start to come in.
- The reviews are pretty positive and once she has 60 reviews she starts her first Pay Per Click Campaign.

B. Stuart's Website Build

Stuart's first product (a set of ceramic knives) has been selling on Amazon for around 4 months and as he is selling 10-15 units a day, he decides that he needs to insure some of this success by registering his Cut Once brand.

He determines that he needs a website to help him get registered and then deliberates over the type of site and why he really needs it.

Stuart decides that the requirement to get brand registered would work with most sites but if he has a purpose built e-commerce site he can use that to expand his business off the Amazon platform.

He pays for twelve months hosting with bluehost.com which includes a free domain name (as Cutonce.com is available he chooses this domain name for his website).

He decides to build his website using Shopify as it is user friendly and easy enough for a layman (someone with limited technical acumen) like him to build a site and maintain it himself.

EXERCISE ELEVEN COMPILE YOUR PRODUCT LAUNCH PLAN

Create a simple marketing plan based on the steps from creating your listing to starting your Pay Per Click campaign.

You should include:

- Creating your listing.

- Creating your discount codes.

- Who will you get to review your product (i.e. specific review groups)?

CHAPTER 11 DIGITAL PRODUCTS.

I'm not saying you will be the next JK Rowling or Tom Clancy but I would feel remiss if I didn't mention e-books as product bonuses or digital products to sell on Kindle.

1. Books to give away

With so many sellers flooding into the market more and more sellers are giving away e books and extra products to make their products more appealing.

You can of course commission a VA to write your e book but unless you provide a detailed brief the finished item may need more work than starting the book from scratch (as I found out with my first product).

a) Whether you write the book or outsource it you need to determine the purpose of the book:
- Is the book designed to promote more use of your product?
  - o Although giving away an e book of lemon drink recipes with a lemon juicer may get more use out of the juicer, the book shouldn't just be an advert for the product.
- Is the book designed to complement the specific category of your product?
  - o Rather than give away a book just for lemon drinks give away a book covering various fruit drinks (this can then be added to multiple fruit related listings).

b) If you are not competent to write the book are you competent to judge the book?
- If you are a budding chef you may be able to write a recipe book or at least be able to write a good scope for your VA to work to.

- o Just because you can cook doesn't mean you can write about it!
- o If you don't feel competent to write or judge a book either reach out to your network for assistance or choose an alternative to an e book (as a product supplement).

2. Your book as a standalone product

The benefits of selling a digital item in Amazon's Kindle department is that you have an unlimited amount of stock (so you don't have to worry about stock replenishment).

Digital products span borders and immediate delivery (worldwide) means that your market has just grown from a potential 330 million in the USA to the world's population.

a) Writing the book yourself

The issue of selling a digital item is that if you are an expert but currently a "nobody" (in the eyes of the media) you may not have anyone that wants to read your book.

If nothing else, writing a free e book may get you into the habit (and teach you the skills to write a Kindle book).

Some people begin writing articles on sites such as ezinearticles.com and when they have enough content they extrapolate that information into a book.

Others have written short stories and poems for their own (and sometimes their children's) amusement and never thought of turning it into a book.

There are no printing costs here and if you suddenly become a digital best seller printing short runs can be the way to turn the book into a physical copy.

Most people will not become a best seller so you shouldn't necessarily depend on this for your only income.

Choose something you are passionate about (or at least knowledgeable about).

If you don't write a best seller or you don't want to sell it on Amazon then you could give your book away as an added value to one of your products.

Just be aware that an e book or any add-on to a physical product should add value to that product. If you don't think that your e book is good enough to sell then you need to determine if it is really a benefit to your product buyer?

3. Outsourcing

There is a lot of time and work required to be a writer and if you are looking at a book as a product rather than writing for your passion I would suggest that writing is not the best use for your time.

There are a few options for outsourcing a book:

- Employ a VA to ghost write a book on a specific product
    - You may find an individual on Elance or Upwork to do this but this can definitely be a case of getting what you pay for.
    - You are unlikely to get a best seller out of this process unless it is a collaboration and you are actually providing your own amazing content.

- Buy the rights to distribute
  - ○ There are suppliers out there that provide e books that you can give away for free (these are usually too generic to provide much benefit to your buyers but can provide you an interim alternative whilst you formulate better add-ons).

EXERCISE TWELVE DETERMINE A DIGITAL PRODUCT

- Define a digital product to give away with your first product
  - ○ Ensure you have a detailed brief of what you want the product to do (e.g. compile 20 recipes with images of Lemons).

- Choose a VA to make the digital product
  - ○ Base the selection on their Bio on Upwork, Fiverr etc.
  - ○ Pick two separate VAs (I suggest that each one is from a separate freelancer site).
  - ○ Commission both VAs to create your product (with a maximum budget of $30 each).
  - ○ Ensure the products have different titles.

- Review the products and choose the best product to launch with your product.
  - ○ If both the products are of an acceptable quality use them both.

- o If using both, promote the best product in the listing and give the second away as a bonus in your second follow up email.

CHAPTER 12 ONGOING MAINTENANCE

Firstly let me say that although an Amazon business may need less time than a corporate 9-5 job it is a business and if that business is not maintained it will fail.

I've provided some questions below (and some answers) to provide some perspective and a bit of direction in this matter.

1. What time do you initially have available for your Amazon business?
- If you are building your business part time you may be limited to the time available but you do need to allocate some specific time (at least once a day).

- The beauty of the 24 hour business is that you can allocate your daily work around your timetable, perhaps an hour after you have put your children to bed etc.

- Although you are setting your own schedule you need to have some flexibility in your timetable for impromptu issues that arise. If you suddenly have an issue with your stock or listing you may have to contact suppliers or Seller central and the time required can suddenly explode to hours (rather than a few minutes).

2. What are some of the ongoing tasks that you are going to require?
- Check your stock levels
  - The stock numbers on Amazon can fluctuate due to returns and various other factors (they aren't perfect) so if you see a discrepancy in your stock levels don't be

afraid to run a report or raise the issue with seller support.

- o Running out of stock is one of the deadliest sins as a seller so you need to keep a track of stock that is fulfillable (available to sell) on your account.
- o Just because your stock has arrived at an FBA warehouse does not make it fulfillable.
- o Although you may ship your stock to one specific FBA Warehouse some units (or all) of your stock may be forwarded to another warehouse and this can add days before that stock is classed as fulfillable.

- Check your sales
  - o Stock levels do not always coincide with sales for various reasons (including returns) so you need to monitor sales to help project stock requirements.

- Check your buyer messages
  - o Answer buyer questions as quickly as possible as this adds to the algorithm that determines the health of your account (in Amazon's eyes!)
  - o Sometimes a buyer message may be a thank you for great service and requires no reply. All messages need to be addressed even if this means just marking them as not requiring a reply.
  - o As the messages can come in at any time it is best to check this at least once a day.

- Check the latest reviews
  - o Because the health of your listing relies so much on reviews it is important to frequently check the rating of your reviews.

- It might not be fair but some competitors purposely coordinate attacks on your account so look for large batches of negative reviews that occur the same day (with little text).

- Address any issues from negative reviews
  - See if the review is genuine and if you believe it is nefarious contact seller support to see if you can get it removed.
  - If a customer has placed a negative review ensure that you address their issues.
  - Confirm that a customer has been offered a refund (if you have to organize the refund, do it.).

- Check your advertising campaigns
  - If your campaign is about to expire amend the expiry date.
  - If your ACOS is at a high percentage look at the keywords and ensure that they are actually relevant to your product.

3. Do you need the cash-flow to order the second lot of stock
- There is a balancing act when you initially launch of having enough stock for demand but limiting the financial cost of your risk.
- If you have limited funds you may need Amazon's payment for your first sales to fund your second bulk order, ensure you take into account:
  - Time required from stock being ordered to sitting at an Amazon warehouse ready to ship to customers.
  - Can you afford any extra stock in your first shipment (with a good launch strategy stock can sell fast so an

extra 100 or so units may make the difference between running out of stock or not).

4. How can you build some insurance into your Amazon business?
- Whether you see your Amazon business as a stepping stone or your final destination it is worth building a safety net such as your own online shop.
- If you set up an e-commerce site such as Shopify you can initially link it to your Amazon seller account and have Amazon distribute your stock from their FBA warehouses.
- Once you have some traction in your online shop you can begin to distribute stock outside the Amazon platform.
- Distributing your stock outside the Amazon system may need an intermediary (especially for overseas sellers) as you may not want to spend time handling stock yourself.
  - There are companies out there (such as GDW) who actually charge less than Amazon to ship and store your products. I estimate that more companies will develop this facility as e-commerce grows.

5. Your sales are plodding along and then suddenly your sales disappear. What can you do?
  - If you have been monitoring your account regularly a sudden halt in sales should stand out to you but don't panic if sales only pause for a day or two.
  - Ensure that you optimize your listing
    - If your competitors have all suddenly dropped their prices you may have to adjust your prices (up or down) and see if that affects your sales.
    - If you have had a few bad reviews (nefarious or not) this may affect your product's review rating.

Look at giving some units to review groups, to regain your star rating.

- o Increase your marketing budget (extra PPC and FB ads etc.) as visibility of your product can improve sales
- Set yourself a time frame for liquidation of the stock (if it isn't selling your stock Is tying up capital).
  - o Ensure you have tried all optimizing steps available to you before you look at cutting your losses.
  - o First option for liquidation is to drop the price of your stock drastically (at this stage you are closing the listing for this product so don't worry about competitors buying your stock and selling at a higher price later). You want to cover the Amazon costs and hopefully make some money
  - o If you have a separate distribution system (e.g. a Shopify store) create a removal order from Amazon and list your products using your own (agents) warehouses.
  - o Create a removal order on you Amazon account and list your item in bulk on Craig's list etc.

6. Are you going to quit your job?
  - As your business grows you may decide at some stage to switch from this being a part time business to your full time income.
    - o You need to decide on your comfort zone (how much of a financial cushion do you need if the business stops dead). 3 months, 6 months, 12 months?
    - o Calculate your monthly needs, include everything from food, insurance and rent, etc. to a lump sum

        for emergencies and a contingency factor (add 10%)

7. Are you going to pay someone to run the business for you?
   - As your business grows and your listings increase you may determine that rather than switching to running the business full time you are going to outsource that part of your business.
   - Just like any business where you delegate duties there has to be some level of trust when you put your business in someone else's hands.
   - Your Amazon Seller account allows you to give individuals restricted access to parts of your account which enables you to delegate tasks (from marketing to stock control).
   - You will need to determine how much control you retain over your account and just like any business you may have to train staff but you can free up time here (and by contracting rather than employing reduce your administration costs).

8. How are you going to prepare for Christmas and Chinese New Year?

The balancing act for stock levels can be a bit of a challenge when you factor in (hopefully) increased sales over the festive season and the fact that Chinese New Year is shortly after the festive season:

- You need to carefully estimate when you will place your order for Christmas stock and how many units you will order.
- A schedule will be required to determine when you will order your replenishment stock (in case you sell large quantities).

- o This requires milestones (e.g. do you reorder when your stock drops from 3000 units to 2000 or when it reaches 1000?).
- o You need to factor in production times and shipping times (realizing that at this time of year both may be extended).
- As Chinese New Year (in 2016 it was in February) can result in all the factories closing down for 2-4 weeks it can have a severe impact on your supply line.
- If you have huge sales over the holiday period you have to estimate when you will place your post-Christmas stock order (and for how many units).
  - o If your sales continued at the same level how much stock would you need to last you over the Chinese New Year disruption.
  - o Depending on the time scale of your supply chain you may need to order two to three months of stock (per item listed).

9. How are you going to track your competitors?
   - Pick the top ten sellers with the same or similar products to yourself.
   - Track their seller ranking and price for a period (this can be done weekly or daily),
   - Use the ASINs to track the products and also ensure their ranking is in the same category as yours
     - o Lots of products look the same so the ASIN is one of the best ways to ensure it is the same product you are tracking
     - o If your product is not in the same category as your competitors' your sales may suffer so I hope that you determined this before launching).

- Check their review status (is their star ranking suddenly dropping).
- Are the images suddenly changing (perhaps your target market is changing)?
- If you notice a trend such as they are all drastically reducing their prices or the ratings on their products are suddenly falling it could be something you need to address
    - Perhaps they have the same supplier and their quality is dropping
    - Perhaps there has been a bad review or a comment in the media on the product.
    - You need to keep on top of your business. Don't just follow your competitors, but be aware that a number of purchasers changing their habits may indicate a new trend.

CASE STUDY

Gregory has launched his first product (a neoprene wrist strap) on Amazon. After the first month he reviews his findings and determines that his 6 initial daily activities will be:

1. Checking his stock

His initial stock order was for 600 units, he's had sales of 300 units and after giving 100 units away for reviews he only has 200 units left in stock.

He determines that his next order should be for 1200 units and contacts his supplier immediately.

2. Checking his sales

His average sales are fifteen units a day with an increase on weekends to twenty five units a day.

He extrapolates these figures out and uses them to project his sales for the next six months.

3. Checking his buyer messages

Over the period of a month he receives eight buyer messages.

Two of the messages were thank you messages for the emails and had to be marked as "not needing a response".

He determined for the time being he will have to check the messages at least once a day to maintain his account health as "Good".

4. Checking his latest reviews

Over a period of three days he notices fifteen one star reviews have been placed on his product, they are all unverified reviews (i.e. they have been placed by people who have not bought his product).

Fearing a competitor attack he contacts Amazon seller Central and raises the issue (after a short investigation Amazon remove the reviews).

5. Addressing any issues from negative reviews

There is a common complaint in the negative reviews that the product smells initially and he addresses this on two fronts:

    a. Contacting the supplier and his inspection company to ensure that the next shipment does not have this strong smell.

    b. Including an insert in (each unit of) his next shipment with instructions to wash the unit thoroughly before using.

6. Checking his advertising campaigns.

His conversion rate for PPC tends to spike at the weekends so he increases his daily budget for Saturdays and Sundays.

He is always looking to grow sales.

EXERCISE THIRTEEN DETERMINE YOUR SIX DAILY AMAZON ACTIVITIES

Here you need six activities that you are going to do on a daily basis (to maintain your Amazon business), suggestions are:

1. Check Payment Summary

2. Check your buyer messages

3. Check your stock

4. Check any advertising campaigns

5. Check your sales and Traffic

6. Check for latest reviews on each listing

With no set schedules you will have to determine your own daily habits. Repetition is recognized as one of the best ways to develop a habit.

It is estimated that a habit can take an average of 66 days to be established (and at least 21 days for an habitual change to take hold). Studies have shown that forming a habit can actually take up to 90 days.

When you take these statistics into consideration documenting your activities initially is probably the best way to ensure that your schedule becomes habitual.

CHAPTER 13 MY LEARNINGS (MISTAKES)

On April 30th 2015 I finished a project management contract and decided to not look for another corporate job – I'd build an Amazon business instead.

I felt that I couldn't write a book on the subject without talking a little about my learnings (mistakes) from the journey so far.

They say that failure is feedback and the feedback I got was that a lot of these mistakes could have been avoided (by not rushing headlong into this situation).

The answers are out there and so many people I have met in my networks are happy to help.

The issue is when you don't know what you don't know so you don't know what questions to ask.

Try to be methodical and not make the same mistake twice.

Some of my learnings:

1. Choosing a product in a restricted category and not knowing this. A newbie error but a mistake I won't make again.

2. Ordering products before setting up a listing, this meant I didn't know about the category (red flags would have risen if I had listed the item before ordering my bulk stock).

3. Because I had a bigger budget I wasn't as frugal with my funds so it took me longer to get my investment back. I set myself $10k for one product and could have easily funded two products from that if I had triple checked before each expenditure (measure twice cut once).

4. Terapeak (the 7 day free trial would have been enough for my initial product research but I paid for 3 months).

5. Not knowing that I could distribute my ebook via feedback genius so setting up an extra email (included in my first product insert) for customers to email me for the book.

6. Commissioning a website for landing pages (suggested by my media VA.) Maybe I wasn't precise enough about what I wanted from my marketing guy but because I wasn't sure from the start about my product launch I paid for domain names, webhosting, another VA to build the site and never touched them.

   - I already had a couple of websites so it was purely the fact that I didn't have a plan that made me waste time, effort and money here.

   - You don't need a website straight away but when you do, decide what you need it for.

   - If you do build a website ensure that you do something for the time or money that you have invested in it. Shopify, WordPress with a shopping basket (as a business card type product so that you can list the contents for your product (Amazon sometimes require this for certain beauty products)).

   - This is why timelines are so important in your budgeting (as it allows reviews).

   - This wasted time with my building content and money on a website I never used.

   - I had built a website myself but didn't analyse my need for a site so got someone else to build it (believing it was a time sensitive issue).

7. Getting a VA on Fiverr to design a logo that was useless and I didn't need as I went for a sports gear logo even before I found a product. Budgets and a business plan would have helped.

8. Not knowing that my product can be classed as needing FDA approval so getting shipments stopped at customs and not allowed into the United States.

9. Getting a VA to produce an ebook as a give-away with my first product that was useless. Even with milestones and a good brief a VA is only as good as their competence level.

10. Thinking that a successful launch will just keep printing money

   - Although Amazon sells 24 hours a day (so you may makes sales whilst you are sleeping) this is not true passive income.

   - You need to monitor both yours and your competitors' listings to react to changes in the market.

   - Although you may have the best product in your category if all of your competitors drop their prices it may affect your sales.

   - When your sales pick up due to a great PPC campaign etc. you may have to increase your marketing budget and not leave it the same.

11. Expecting suppliers to meet the initial timelines. They promise the earth to get the order but aren't always as diligent at achieving deadlines.

12. Not addressing negative reviews

   - Even if you give a refund some customers will post a negative review.

- Some of the negative reviews are nefarious (placed by competitors) and they are just a fact of doing business.

- You can reduce a percentage of negative feedback with good service (Feedback Genius etc. allows contact from customers).

- Answering customers reviews with a confirmation that they can get a refund can help foster good relations (be sure you don't break Amazon's T&Cs).

13. Not factoring in the time from the product landing in the States to being available on Amazon's shelves. You may think that once the product hits the States it is available but you also need to factor:

- Time for processing.

- Shipping time in the USA.

- Processing time at Amazon.

Don't be scared to make mistakes

I understand that the mistakes that we remember are usually the ones we make ourselves and not the ones we have read about but hopefully by reading what I have done you can learn a little from my mistakes and make fewer yourself.

EXERCISE FOURTEEN LIST YOUR MISTAKES

In previous chapters I have given a case study for guidance in that chapter's exercise. In this chapter I was the case study.

1. Start a list of the mistakes that you make during your Amazon journey.

2. Feel free to write my mistakes on your list so that you don't make the same mistakes.

Add to your list as you go through the process and include remarks or comments of actions that you can undertake to avoid making the same mistakes again.

CHAPTER 14 EXERCISE SUMMARY

EXERCISE ONE DEFINE YOUR WHY (AND PRINT IT OFF)

In order to determine your WHY it is important to focus on your values and determine WHY you undertake any task.

The stronger your emotional WHY, the easier it will be for you to work through any speed bumps in your Amazon business.

There are whole books and courses devoted to setting your WHY (some mentioned in the glossary section at the end of this book) so don't be too disheartened if your first attempt at this exercise doesn't fill you with excitement.

If you work through the WHY exercise and read the next couple of chapters but don't feel your WHY is strong enough, don't let this stop you taking action to build an Amazon business. Avoid Analysis Paralysis.

Assuming you are not looking at building a business just for fun, the main reason you are building an Amazon business is probably what the profits earned will allow you to do; so let's explore that a little more.

STEP 1

1. Pick one major reason WHY you need the funds from an Amazon Business

Some of the reasons why people look at an Amazon business are:

- As a supplementary income
  - To pay for their education.

- To pay for luxuries (e.g. a sports car or a speed boat).

- To fund other investment opportunities.

- As an alternative to their current job that they hate (to give them more time flexibility).

- As a stepping stone to a larger investment opportunity.

If you are a parent, there is probably nothing that you wouldn't give for your child's happiness (including a limb or your life). So a WHY of paying for your children's education may work for a parent, but a single teenager would have a different WHY.

Although some people may not be motivated by having more possessions, there is nothing wrong with wanting a better life for yourself. A young entrepreneur may be driven more by fast cars and speed boats.

Whatever stage of life you are at, having a WHY of just wanting to pay your bills may initially seem like a strong driving force; but it can be hard to get passionate about a grocery bill. IF you can, find a WHY that is more compelling.

STEP 2

2. If you are finding it difficult to determine a WHY in relation to the benefits of building a business then focus on what would happen if you didn't build a business.

- Imagine the pain of not achieving your goals (e.g. seeing your children's sadness that you missed their performances).

- Now reverse those thoughts by imagining the joy of achieving your goal (e.g. seeing your children's happy face that you attended their performances) and focus on this positive.

There are some schools of thought out there that state that we are motivated more by the avoidance of pain than by thoughts of pleasure. Personally I believe that we gravitate towards what we focus on.

Once you have used this reversal process and determined your WHY, focus only on the positive outcomes.

STEP 3

3. Condense your WHY into a sentence

- e.g. I NEED TO EARN MONEY FROM AN AMAZON BUSINESS SO THAT I CAN QUIT MY CORPORATE JOB AND ATTEND ALL OF MY CHILDREN'S ACTIVITIES

- If you have a huge WHY that you feel you could write a whole book about, distil it down to the strongest sentence (the essence) that inspires your emotions.

- An Amazon business can have large earning potential so don't be afraid to have a huge WHY (funding an orphanage overseas or some other bigger legacy).

STEP 4

4. Close your eyes and repeat that sentence (you created in step 2) at least a dozen times.

- How does it makes you feel?

- Does that sentence excite you?

- If your WHY isn't strong enough to excite you then work through the exercise again.

Anthony Robbins states that "people who have trouble achieving their goals are working off impotent goals". A strong WHY is the driving force for your goals so don't start with an impotent WHY!

STEP 5

5. Keep your WHY with you as your driving force. People have various methods of reminding themselves of their WHY:

- An enlarged version of the sentence in a picture frame (some people keep that frame in their office or bedroom) somewhere prominent.

- Written on a laminated card in their purse/ wallet or somewhere readily available.

- A tattoo of the sentence (this can be a bit extreme and as your WHY may change through life and I do advise against this).

STEP 6

6. If you find that your initial WHY isn't strong enough then feel free to utilize any of the following resources to help you refine it:

- "Getting to the Why" – a book by JB Symons.

- "Roadblocks to Goal Setting" – a book (and audio course) by Morris Goodman.

- "Get the Edge" – a seven day audio course by Anthony Robbins.

- "Creating Your Perfect Lifestyle" – a book by Oli Hille.

Although I would ask that you do not wait for the perfect WHY before proceeding to the next chapter (you can refine that later) I would advise having some form of WHY before you proceed.

Just as it's difficult to hit a goal when you don't know what you are aiming at, it can be difficult to remain motivated in any endeavour if you don't know why you are doing it.

Your WHY may change through life which is why the young entrepreneur and the old retiree may have different WHYs.

EXERCISE TWO CALCULATING OPPORTUNITY COSTS

You are going to input the details into a table so this exercise can be done via spreadsheet, MS Word table or even drawing a table with pen and paper.

I.   For any opportunity we will start by completing column A with the annual hours we will require to invest in that opportunity.

II. Now input the amount of cash required to invest in the opportunity into column B.

III. Multiplying the hours (in column A) times 10 to give us a dollar value and add this to the funds required to give you the total investment (put this in column C).

IV. Now input your estimated potential yearly revenue for the opportunity in column D. We are going to use a ball park figure for the potential return on our investment but before you invest any money in an investment I implore you to crunch the numbers in more detail.

V.   You need to determine how risky you view the investment (based on your risk tolerance) but input the corresponding number from the values above into column E.

VI.   We are now going to calculate the potential to see if the opportunity is worth pursuing.

    a.   Take the figure **D** divide by **C** divide by **E.**

    b.   Multiply your answer by **100** and round up to the next whole number.

    c.   The final multiplication step is purely to give you some whole numbers (as individuals can more easily visualize whole numbers).

VII.   Because you are aiming for a high potential return, if you are receiving a low return on your investment, it is important to recognise that that is stopping you from generating a greater potential return on the same investment (therefore a low return has a higher opportunity cost).

VIII.   The higher the potential figure (in column F) the lower the opportunity cost, the lower the figure the higher the opportunity cost.

Opportu nity	Hours Req'd ($10/h)	Funds Req'd ($)	Total Invest ment ($)	Potentia l R.O.I. ($)	Risk	Poten tial
	A	B	C	D	E	F
Savings Account	0	$10,000	$10,000	$500	2	3
Hedge Fund	200	$3,000	$5,000	$10,000	4	50
Online Biz	1000	$5,000	$15,000	$100,000	6	111
Your Opportu nity						

EXERCISE THREE SET A FINANCIAL BUDGET

Set yourself a financial budget (using the information in the table above as a guideline).

How much money are you prepared to risk in this venture?

You don't need all of the funds at the start. As you will see in the timeline chapter various funds will be required at different stages of the process.

We are just looking at a financial budget here (time required in exchange for potential earnings was covered previously in the opportunity costs).

- How much cash have you got available (including potential credit) and based on the information below is it enough?

- Your budget can take into account potential revenue (from sales) before ordering new stock etc.

- You may decide to launch one product at a time or six but you do need to have an idea if your budget will cover your decision.

EXERCISE FOUR YOUR EDUCATION

In the last chapter you set yourself a budget (I do hope you included an Education Fund in there).

As the theme of this book is condensing info it would be wrong of me to have you following hundreds of people (as each teacher has their own different style).

I want you to look at the resources out there (feel free to look at the resources mentioned here and in the resources chapter).

1. Choose two mentors (in the ecommerce field) whose information you will focus on in detail. Remember you are after their information and don't necessarily need to contact them.

2. Choose at least one course (it can be free) that you will undertake in the next 30 days.

3. Join at least two networks (Facebook groups etc.) that are focussed on Amazon Selling / e commerce.

4. Read this book to the end (you've paid for it so use it).

EXERCISE FIVE WRITE A BUSINESS PLAN

This doesn't need to be as long as war and peace but should include some of the basics below:

- A Financial plan

- A structure for your business,

- A potential business timetable.

- A list of your products

Some of us are big picture people and some of us are very detailed so try to avoid waiting for the perfect business plan before you start your business.

Most business plans are like a living thing and will evolve with time.

EXERCISE SIX SET YOURSELF A TIMELINE FOR YOUR FIRST LAUNCH

I've provided a case study above to give you some guidance and you can adapt this to meet your own requirements.

Remember:

- The product research period may take longer than you intend but it is time well spent.

- You may be waiting four weeks or so for a product to be ready to fulfil customer orders (so fill that time wisely).

- If you have any time available whilst you are waiting for products try to get ahead with any upcoming tasks.

EXERCISE SEVEN COMPILE AND CATEGORIZE A LIST OF ACTIVITIES

The activities needed to get you from your current status to the stage where your product is available for sale on Amazon (feel free to use the timelines exercise in chapter five to help you with this list).

1. Once you have completed your activities list categorize it into which activities you are going to outsource and which activities you are going to undertake yourself.

2. Start investigating sources for the activities that you have decided to outsource.

EXERCISE EIGHT START YOUR PRODUCT RESEARCH

1. Create a list of at least 100 products that you believe meet your criteria.

2. Narrow that list down to three products with the best potential (and profit margins).

3. Determine which of your chosen products you will contact suppliers for quotes

- Don't be afraid to have real time chats (with suppliers) to gather the information in estimating shipping rates etc.

- If you do start chatting at these early stages be professional and leave yourself an out (telling a supplier you need to get permission to make a decision is not a sign of weakness and allows you the chance to contact them again for further information).

Summary

You have been estimating your costs and calculations on the product prices (and MOQs) listed on alibaba.com.

You should now have a shortlist of products ranging from 3-10 products

Assuming that you have estimated most of your costs to get the product from a factory in China to Amazon's warehouse and that there is still enough profit margin in your product you now need detailed costings.

In the next chapter we will focus on your dealings with suppliers and helping you find one.

EXERCISE NINE CONFIRM YOUR FIRST PRODUCT FOR LAUNCH

- Contact at least three suppliers of that product on Alibaba and negotiate the best deal you can for a shipment of 1000 (do not place the order for 1000 units!).

- Order a sample of 10-15 sample units of your chosen product (from at least one supplier).

- If your product will be Private labelled you want to try get sample PLs (especially if you are an overseas buyer).

EXERCISE TEN SET UP A DUMMY LISTING

Setting up your listing may seem daunting but you don't know if you can until you try.

I suggest that you try a listing before you outsource this task.

Ideally pick the item you are going to launch and work through the listing process.

In Seller Central type "List your first item" in the search box.

In the search results you will find "Video Tutorial List your first item". Follow the tutorial and fill in the details for your first product (you can always delete this practice listing later so don't worry that you need to use this to list your first product).

There are lots of tutorial videos in Seller Central and they're (free) updated if Amazon change their system.

EXERCISE ELEVEN COMPILE YOUR PRODUCT LAUNCH PLAN

Create a simple marketing plan based on the steps from creating your listing to starting your Pay Per Click campaign.

You should include:

- Creating your listing

- Creating your discount codes

- Who will you get to review your product (i.e. specific review groups)

EXERCISE TWELVE DETERMINE A DIGITAL PRODUCT

- Define a digital product to give away with your first product

- o Ensure you have a detailed brief of what you want the product to do (e.g. compile 20 recipes (with images) of Lemons.

- Choose a VA to make the digital product

  - o Base the selection on their Bio on Upwork, Fiverr etc.

  - o Pick two separate VAs (I suggest that each one is from a separate freelancer site).

  - o Commission both VAs to create your product (with a maximum budget of $30 each).

  - o Ensure the products have different titles.

- Review the products and choose the best product to launch with your product.

  - o If both the products are of an acceptable quality use them both.

  - o If using both, promote the best product in the listing and give the second away as a bonus in your second follow up email.

EXERCISE THIRTEEN DETERMINE YOUR SIX DAILY AMAZON ACTIVITIES

Here you need six activities that you are going to do on a daily basis (to maintain your Amazon business), suggestions are:

1. Check Payment Summary

2. Check your buyer messages

3. Check your stock

4. Check any advertising campaigns

5. Check your sales and Traffic

6. Check for latest reviews on each listing

With no set schedules you will have to determine your own daily habits. Repetition is recognized as one of the best ways to develop a habit.

It is said that a habit can take an average of 66 days (and 21 days to make a change) but a habit can take up to 90 days so documenting your activities initially is probably the best way to ensure that you build that habit.

EXERCISE FOURTEEN LIST YOUR MISTAKES

In previous chapters I have given a case study for guidance in that chapter's exercise. In this chapter I was the case study.

1. Start a list of the mistakes that you make during your Amazon journey.

2. Feel free to write my mistakes on your list so that you don't make the same mistakes.

Add to your list as you go through the process and include remarks or comments of actions that you can undertake to avoid making the same mistakes again.

CHAPTER 15 GLOSSARY

I understand that a lot of the terms here are common tongue to most but as this book is aimed at a broad spectrum of readers I have tried to be as inclusive as possible.

At the time of writing this book the information included below is current but I accept no responsibility for changes of external sites and sources at a later date.

A

A SALES TAX NEXUS

A Nexus (also called "sufficient physical presence,") is a legal term that refers to the requirement for companies doing business in a state to collect and pay tax on sales in that state.

ALGORITHM

A set of steps in mathematics (and computer science) that are performed to provide the results of a calculation or automated reasoning task. The steps are performed in a set process and in relation to computers are followed automatically.

ALIBABA (an abbreviation of Alibaba.com)

The biggest online commerce company in China that encompasses its three websites Taobao, Tmall and Alibaba.com

AMAZON (an abbreviation of Amazon.com,)

The largest online retailer in the United States and the parent company of various other Amazon online retailers such as Amazon.co.uk in the UK.

AMAZON'S SEARCH ALGORITHM

The calculation that Amazon uses from various factors (on its website) to determine popularity of a product and various other details about its product's listing.

AMZTRACKER

A keyword Tracker available from AMZTRACKER.com.

ANALYSIS PARALYSIS

The art of spending so much time analysing an opportunity that you don't actually have any progress in that opportunity.

ANCHORING

The act of basing your judgement on a familiar reference point, by focusing on a specific thought or place we can psychologically anchor to that point when our views and beliefs are tested.

ASIN (Amazon Standard Identification Number)

A ten character alpha numeric indicator that Amazon uses to identify individual items in its catalogue.

B

BIO (Biography)

A detailed description of someone's life, online biographies tend to be more abridged than actual books written as biographies and tend to focus on specific activities the person has done in relation to an article, course or product.

BITLY (Bitly.com)

A website designed to reduce the size of your URLs.

BLOG (abbreviated from weblog)

A regularly updated website or web page written in a more informal, conversational style than more traditional websites.

BLOGGER

A person who updates a blog (frequently).

BLUEHOST (an abbreviation of Bluehost.com)

A large web hosting service based in the USA.

BRAND

A brand is a type of product manufactured by a particular company under a particular name (e.g. Coca cola).

BRAND REGISTRY

A service provided by Amazon that allows its sellers to register their informal brands in order to protect their listings from being hijacked.

BRICKS AND MORTAR SELLER

A term traditionally describing a retail shop that sells its products from a physical building. You go into a bricks and mortar shop and buy the products you see whereas for an online shop you look at an online version of the product and have it shipped to you.

BULK ORDER

A large order placed on a supplier (usually 500 units or more).

BUYER BEWARE

A well-known legal warning that notifies the buyer that the goods he or she is buying are subject to all defects.

BUYER MESSAGES

Messages posted in your Seller Central Dashboard through Amazon.com.

C

CASHFLOW

The financial capital flowing in and out of your accounts (positive Cashflow means you have more coming in than going out).

CATEGORY

The Specific area of the Amazon site that a product is listed in (e.g. a tire may be listed in the Automotive Category).

CHARITY

An organization that exists to serve a charitable mission.

COPYRIGHT

Copyright legally protects your original works like artwork, books, computer programs, drawings, films, music and sound recordings. You may use the symbol © to help you demonstrate that you claim copyright in a particular work. Your protection is free and applies automatically from the work's creation (in most cases it applies for your lifetime plus 50 years).

CRAIG'S LIST

An online version of the old classified ad. The site allows buyers and sellers to connect to exchange products or services (throughout the USA).

CODESCHOOL (Codeschool.com)

A website for coding instruction of HTML or various other coding languages.

CODE

Used as an abbreviation for computer code or computer languages.

CODING

The art of creating computer programs, apps or other digital creations using computer languages.

COLONEL SANDERS

An American businessman best known for founding the fast food chicken restaurant Kentucky Fried Chicken. Sanders is seen as an inspiration for older people as (after failing 1009 times) he didn't become successful until he was 65.

COPY AND PASTE

A well know term for the functions in word processing software such as MS Word, you highlight the text in one document (or application) and copy that text into another document (or application). This is the modern version of scrapbooking where a pair of scissors and a glue stick have been replaced with a computer mouse.

CERTIFIED PUBLIC ACCOUNTANT (CPA)

A financial accountant who has qualified and is licensed by one of the fifty US States.

CREATING YOUR PERFECT LIFESTYLE

A book by Oli Hille of the Anthony Robbins genre. The book includes lots of great resources for working on your goals and your WHY.

COMMA SEPARATED VALUES (CSV)

A digital format used to store tabular data (such as spreadsheets or database files).

CUSTOMS (Abbreviated from Customs and Excise)

When goods are imported into a country there is sometimes a government tax (also known as Excise) that has to be paid before the items can be legally brought into the country.

D

DOMAIN NAME (Also known as Domain)

A domain name is what you type into a browser to find a website. They are basically digital addresses on the internet and are usually leased on an annual basis.

DUMMY LISTING

A practice or superfluous listing that you create with the intention to delete it without using it as a live listing.

E

EFT (Emotion Free Techniques) often known as Tapping or EFT Tapping.

A universal healing tool that can provide impressive results for physical, emotional, and performance issues.

https://www.youtube.com/playlist?list=PLl1nvgT4Uv8KqoKsdSFbY emkPqxV_5PfD

ELANCE (abbreviated from Elance.com)

An online staffing platform based in Mountain View, California, United States operated by Upwork where individuals can contract freelancers for tasks.

EMPLOYER IDENTIFICATION NUMBER (EIN)

A unique nine digit number allocated by the IRS (of the USA) to businesses for the purpose of identification.

F

FACEBOOK

A social networking website that makes it easy for you to connect and share with your family and friends online.

FBA INSPECTIONS (fbainspections.com)

A private company based out of California that provides preparation and repackaging of products to send to Amazon fulfilment warehouses (amongst other services).

FEEDBACK GENIUS (feedbackgenius.com)

A software sold by Seller Labs that allows you to automatically converse (and distribute digital products) to your Amazon customers.

FULFILLED BY AMAZON (FBA)

When Amazon is fulfilling your stock they take care of the warehousing, distribution and revenue collection for your product.

FIVERR (an abbreviation for Fiverr.com)

An online platform where you can hire freelancers to carry out almost any activity that can be performed on a computer. The title comes from the fact that you can hire people for tasks starting as low as five US Dollars.

FKNSU

In order to identify individual products on the enormous Amazon inventory the Amazon system allocates a separate code to each individual product listing. That individual code is known as the FKNSU.

FLICKR (flickr.com)

An image and video hosting website that was created by Ludicorp in 2004 and purchased by Yahoo in 2005.

FOOD FOR THOUGHT

A term used to relate to mental stimulation or mental nourishment.

FULFILLABLE

When this term is used in relation to an Amazon listing it means your stock is available to be sold and distributed out to customers.

G

GDW (gdwinc.com)

A private company based out of Houston Texas that has been involved in online retail for over 15 years. They provide preparation and repackaging of products to send to Amazon fulfilment warehouses (amongst other services).

GETTING TO THE WHY

A book by JB Symons (available in hard copy or via kindle) that provides detailed guidance for defining your why.

GET THE EDGE

A Seven Day Audio course by Anthony Robbins (available through AnthonyRobbins.com) that provides detailed guidance for personal development including goal setting and defining your why.

GOOGLE CHROME

Is a Web browser.

GOOGLE CHROME EXTENSION

A piece of software that can be added to the google chrome platform (an extension) that allows you to get extra functions out of Google Chrome.

H

HIJACKING YOUR LISTING

Similar to piggybacking but this time another Amazon seller is selling a product different to your product against your listing (this is against Amazon's Terms of Service)

HOSTGATER (Hostgater.com)

A large web hosting service based in the USA.

HOT LEAD

In marketing terms when an individual is classified as a hot lead it means that they are very interested in buying your product.

HTML (Hyper Text Markup language)

A standardized system used to format text when building websites or creating content on the worldwide web.

I

INCOME TAX

The tax levied by a government against income earned as an individual or from a business.

INSTAGRAM (an abbreviation of Instagram.com)

An online mobile photo-sharing, video-sharing, and social networking service that enables its users to take pictures and videos, and share them either publicly or privately on the app, as well as through a variety of other social networking platforms, such as Facebook, Twitter, Tumblr, and Flickr.

INTERNAL REVENUE SERVICE (IRS)

A government bureau of the Treasury department of the United States of America responsible for tax collection.

J

JUNGLE SCOUT

This is a paid Google Chrome extension sold by a company through their website Junglescout.com. It allows you to analyse product listing information (when searching on Amazon.com through the Google chrome browser).

K

KEYWORD

In relation to a search on Amazon.com the keyword is a word or term typed into the search box when trying to find an item in the Amazon catalogue. If you know what the keywords are that your potential customers are using for searches you can adapt your listing to include those words.

KEYWORDINSPECTOR (an abbreviation of keywordinspector.com)

Keyword inspector allows you to use the tool on your competitors (just inputting their ASIN) and it will give you a CSV file showing all the keywords they are listed for.

L

LISTING (An abbreviation of Amazon Seller Listing)

In order for customers to find products on Amazon the items need to be listed in Amazon's digital catalogue. The listing includes all the information about a product that the seller has input including images and pricing.

LOGO

This can be a symbol a mark or graphic mark commonly used by an organization to make them instantly public recognized. Great examples are the blue bird used by Twitter or the golden M of MacDonald's.

M

MARK SCOTT ADAMS

Mark is a gentleman who has built many businesses (bricks and mortar and online) over the years. Mark provides some great resources on his site Markscottadams.com. The course info is at http://MarkScottAdams.com/fre-training and the course is at http://FBAheadstart.com.

MARK ZUCKERBERG

The American computer programmer, internet entrepreneur and philanthropist who created Facebook at a very early age.

MENTOR

A mentor is traditionally defined as a professional relationship (although most mentors affect lifestyles and not just work) where an experienced individual provides knowledge, support and encouragement to help an individual meet their potential.

MERCHANTWORDS (an abbreviation of merchantwords.com).

A company that provides products that analyse the keywords most used to search for products on Amazon.com (to assist in you marketing).

MERIDIAN POINT

A specific point on the body thought to be the end of energy paths (meridians) throughout the body.

MONEY MASTERY THE GAME

A book by Anthony Robbins that provides guidance and in depth financial research into the American finance industry. Great information on costs incurred for individuals' Investments.

MONEY POOR

A term that means what it says, you do not have enough money available to meet your requirements.

MINIMUM ORDER QUANTITY – MOQ

The minimum order quantity. In the manufacturing world it is usually more cost effective to manufacture a larger quantity of products (in a production run), these reduced costs can sometimes be passed on to wholesale buyers. The cost of smaller numbers in a production run can also be less cost effective and these costs can also be passed onto a wholesale buyer. By setting a minimum order quantity the manufacturer is stating that a production run of a lesser quantity would not be profitable for them.

MICROSOFT (MS) WORD

A word processing software product sold by the Microsoft Company.

N

NEON LIGHTS Review Group

An independent review group based on Facebook that provides a free service to review your discounted products.

O

OPPORTUNITY COSTS

This relates to the potential costs (in time or money) that you are incurring by investing in a specific endeavour. If you invested $100 in a lottery ticket and didn't win the cost would be your $100 stake plus any potential revenue that you could have made from investing that money elsewhere.

OUTSOURCING

This is the act where an external individual (or company) is contracted by one company to undertake tasks that would normally be done within the first company. If you are a sole trader you are the company that is contracting others to carry out those tasks.

P

PAYPAL (an abbreviation of PayPal.com)

An online payment service that securely allows you to buy products online with added protection.

PAY PER CLICK (PPC)

An auction type system for an internal advertising platform on Amazon.com. Customers input words in their searches for products and if you have a winning bid in that word's auction your

Ads show up. You pay the amount that you have bid if the customer then clicks on your product Ad.

PIESNERJOHNSON (piesnerjohnson.com)

A CPA company based in the USA Specializing in sales tax peisnerjohnson.com.

PIGGY BACKING

When another Amazon seller sells the same item as you (on the Amazon platform) under your listing it.

PINTEREST (pinterest.com)

A social network that allows users to visually share, and discover new interests by posting Images or videos to their own or others' boards.

PRIVATE LABEL (PL)

The act of changing or adapting a product generally (available for sale) so that it is now classed as your own product. An action as simple as adding your own logo to a product can class it as privately labelled. This activity is normally carried out to differentiate your products on Amazon to avoid your listing being hijacked.

PRODUCT LAUNCH

The process and timeframe where you initially begin to sell your product on Amazon.

PRODUCT SAMPLES

The initial units of your product that you order from your supplier in order to gauge the quality and reliability of your supplier.

PROFIT MARGIN

The difference between the purchase price (including any additional intermediary costs) and the profit left over after all sales costs are deducted.

R

RANKING

Traditionally a ranking is a relationship between two or more items (think your top ten favourite songs of all time). In this book ranking refers to the ranking of a product on Amazon.com in relation to other products listed on Amazon.

REDDIT (Reddit.com)

An entertainment, social news networking service and news website.

RETAIL ARBITRAGE (RA)

The act of purchasing the same product that is listed on Amazon from a bricks and mortar shop (at a discount) and selling that product against the listing on Amazon for a profit. The Amazon app makes it easy for individuals to check the price that the shop is selling against the price that Amazon are selling the same product for.

REVIEW KICK (reviewkick.com)

An independent company that provides reviewers for your discounted products.

REVIEWS (short for Customer reviews)

Written feedback placed against your Amazon listing (either positive or negative) that contributes to the ranking of your product listing.

RINSE and REPEAT

A term referring to carrying out the same set of actions in a set sequence repeatedly.

ROADBLOCKS TO GOAL SETTING

A book (and audio course) by Morris Goodman which can help you with goal setting and ultimately your WHY.

RETURN ON INVESTMENT (R.O.I.)

A ratio calculating how much money was made on an investment as a percentage of the purchase price.

S

SALES TAX

A tax levied by an American state against the purchaser of a particular product (similar to UK VAT, New Zealand GST etc.)

SALES TAX NEXUS

The Nexus is technically (also known as sufficient physical presence) the determining factor of whether an out-of-state business selling products into a state is liable for collecting sales or use tax on sales into the state. You need to know if you have a sales nexus in a state to determine whether or not to register for sales tax in that state.

SHOPIFY (Abbreviation of Shopify.com)

A website that allows you to setup an online store with very little technical knowhow. The system allows you to build your own ecommerce site as it comes with all the tools for a customer to buy your products.

SOCIAL ENTERPRISE

An organization that applies commercial strategies to maximize improvements in human and environmental well-being.

STARTUP BROS

Will Mitchell and Kyle Eschenroeder (also known as the Startup bros) are passionate entrepreneurs who have been obsessed with business and the internet since birth. Providing courses and mentorship through resources such as startupbros.com.

STOCK

The units of your product that you physically own. Can refer to stock you have purchased from your supplier that is in transit or stock that Amazon is storing for you to sell.

SUPER URL

A specific online link that is designed to take you to a specific item listed on Amazon.com via an automatic set of pathways. Because this can be termed as manipulating the Amazon algorithm it can be seen as breaching their terms of service.

SUPPLIER

A term for the company supplying your product that can encompass the manufacturer or an agent who buys from a manufacturer.

T

TAX JAR (Taxjar.com)

A company providing a software system that automates your sales tax reporting for your Amazon listings.

TERAPEAK (Terapeak.com)

Terapeak is a product that is useful for determining the amount of competition for a product on EBay which can help in determining the market for that product on Amazon.com.

TERMS OF SERVICE

In relation to Amazon the terms of service are the rules and regulations that you must adhere to in order to buy or sell through the Amazon website. Individuals who have fallen foul of these rules when selling on Amazon have also had their ability to purchase other items from Amazon revoked.

THE AMAZON GODS

A term I use to cover the Amazon processes and guidelines that govern all the aspects of selling on Amazon. It can seem as though the decisions that the people and processes make about your listings are irrational and that they have the power of god over your ability to sell your products.

TIME POOR

A term that means what it says, you do not have enough time available to meet your requirements.

TINYURL.COM

A website to reduce the size of your URLs (amongst other things).

TRADE ASSURANCE

A free payment protection service from Alibaba.com. Highly advisable to use this system when purchasing through Alibaba as in most cases they are very reliable in settling disputes with suppliers.

TRADEMARK

A symbol, logo word or words that are legally registered to represent a company (e.g. Coca Cola or Disney). You cannot sell products with a registered trademark without the written permission of the owner of those trademark rights.

TUMBLR (tumblr.com)

A microblogging platform and social networking website that allows you to post multimedia and other content in a short form blog.

TWITTER (twitter.com)

An online social networking service that enables users to send and receive messages no longer than 140 characters long.

U

UNITS

A standard measurement equivalent to one item of a particular product (when ordering from suppliers the items tend to be referred to by number of units).

UNGATING

The process of getting clearance to sell in a restricted category on Amazon.com.

UNIVERSAL PRODCUT CODE (UPC)

A sequence of twelve numerical digits that are uniquely assigned to each trade item. Usually displayed as a barcode that can be scanned throughout the distribution service and allow tracking of an item.

UPWORK (Upwork.com)

An online platform where you can hire freelancers to carry out almost any activity that can be performed on a computer.

UNIFORM RESOURCE LOCATOR (URL)

A direct link to an online address. Usually displayed in blue font and underlined, clicking on this link takes you to a specific place on the internet.

V

VA - Virtual Assistant

A person that you contract to do specific activities (e.g. photo editing). They are sometimes overseas and you may never meet the assistant in person.

V-TRUST (Vtrust.com)

An independent inspection company offering services in China, India and Vietnam.

W

WEB BROWSER

Also known as a browser this is software that is used to access the internet.

WEBINAR

Simplistically a webinar is a seminar conducted over the internet (abridged from the words Seminar and Worldwide web).

WEEBLY (Weebly.com)

A web hosting service that provides its own simple system to allow you to build websites.

WIRE TRANSFER

A digital way of transferring funds between two parties (can be via banks or western union type financial).

WIX (Wix.com)

A web hosting service that provides its own simple system to allow you to build websites.

WORDPRESS

A web hosting service that provides its own simple system to allow you to build websites.

WEB HOSTING

Web hosting means that the digital information for your website is being (hosted) stored somewhere. Companies such as Bluhost.com provide storage spaces for that digital information (known as servers).

Y

YOUTUBE (YouTube.com)

A video sharing platform where you can display a video or view a video others have created. This platform has videos of everything from kittens playing a piano to instructions for you to build a cabin out of logs.

40084238R00115